MAKE IT and TAKE IT

Homemade Gear for Camp and Trail   •   by Russ Mohney
Drawings by the author

Pacific Search Press/craft

To Harriet Bullitt and Sid Rice, who gave their support and
encouragement while I hammered out this book, who share with me a love and
appreciation of the wilderness, and who practice
do-it-yourself tinkering on the grandest of scales!

Pacific Search Press, 715 Harrison Street, Seattle, Washington 98109
© 1977 by Pacific Search Press. All rights reserved
Manufactured in the United States of America

Second printing 1978

Designed by Pamela Hoffman
Edited by Deborah Easter

Library of Congress Cataloging in Publication Data
Mohney, Russ.
    Make it and take it.

    1. Camping—Outfits, supplies, etc.   2. Handicraft.
I. Title.
GV191.76.M6   688.7'6'5   77-14299
ISBN 0-914718-25-8 pbk.

Cover: Russ Mohney camping at Denny Creek in Washington State.
Pictured gear you can make includes: doggie pack, boot hanger, backpack tent,
sleeping pad, gaiter, loss-proof sheath, camera hitch, Alaskan packboard,
all-purpose packsack, stripping basket, classic fly book, nylon utility bag,
ax sheath, fish fillet board, backpack grill, cascade cup, backpack oven.
Photo by Bernard Nist.

Contents

Doing It Yourself

The art and science of "taking to the wilderness" has always been the ideal of a special group of people. From the first explorers and pioneers who crossed the American continent to the recreational backpackers, weekend hikers, and ardent anglers of today—these people have stood apart from the mainstream of their society. They have been characterized as nonconformists, dreamers, or even as dangerous to the complacency of civilized life.

Shunning the early comforts of the infant cities, the first errant types crossed the borders of darkness and entered an unknown land. Judged by contemporary social standards, they suffered hardships, but seemed unaware of the differences between their lives and those of the settled farmers and businessmen they had left behind. In fact, these pioneers *adapted* to the more rigorous life of the frontier—and they would not have traded it for anything!

Even as recently as a century ago, many people still had an intimate relationship with nature as their livelihood was dependent on working the soil beneath them. It took a particularly salty type to first conceive of *recreation*, of *fun*, as shouldering a pack and heading deeper into those everyday woods. Yet a surprising number of souls did just that.

Having inherited some of the adaptable spirit of the original pioneers, these recreational nomads developed a few of the portable comforts we all enjoy today, and passed on their nomadic spirit to the present generation of outdoor wanderers. Today, as hikers, we impose the rigors and hardships of the wilderness on ourselves to a lesser degree. Temporarily casting aside the creature comforts of society, we thrust ourselves headlong into the open land, anticipating and relishing the differences we find there. Even though such "roughing it" is now a temporary phenomenon, the outdoor person still exhibits that peculiar flexibility that has always been a hallmark of our ilk. We have been known to fix a flapping boot sole with monofilament fishing line, repair a leaky tent with a wad of gum, and cook our morning gruel in a birch-bark cone. It has been accurately said that an experienced hiker can fix anything with absolutely nothing, and can mend everything except the crack of dawn! These "idiosyncrasies" never change.

Although the modern backpacker is not especially luxury oriented (if so he would have stayed at home!), practically everyone has adopted a few bits of comfort in hiking and camping. Of course, we all realize that a handful of spartan backpackers take a certain perverse pleasure in finding just how barely they can exist. After all, it is quite possible to spend a week in the woods with nothing more than the clothes on our backs, a mouthful of anonymous granola for sustenance, and a tattered cover to ward off the evening chill. Yet, it is equally possible to spend a week along the wilderness trail with an enormous degree of comfort, safety, and a gourmet menu for every meal. Regardless of the degree of comfort you desire, it is the choice of equipment that makes the difference in the quality of the experience.

The task of collecting all the little gadgets and gimcracks a modern backpacker "needs" may be a trifle taxing to the purse and even more of a burden to the back; after all, if you plan to use it, you must get it out there! Most experienced hikers have gradually built up an inventory of equipment on the basis of need. We have decided that we can get along nicely without grandpa's old cast-iron skillet, and substitute a lightweight aluminum model instead. We have overcome the temptation to dash through the outfitter's shop, grabbing at every shiny little accessory that strikes our fancy. We have, in short, determined which of several million pieces of gear we really need to ensure a safe and memorable outing.

To build up a backpacking inventory at minimal cost, many hikers have fashioned, at home, gear that serves a multitude of purposes. This do-it-yourself urge in the outdoorsman is usually a response learned over the years, punctuated by necessity and a skinny purse. Some may say our frugality teeters on the edge of fanaticism, but then so does our honest desire to enhance the wilderness experience we have chosen!

Another incentive for making our own equipment is that often what we want just is not being sold. Even though the shelves are lined with such exotic devices as a combination can opener, bottle brush, and tent-peg sharpener, it is virtually impossible to go out and *buy* custom-fitted bags for a thousand odds and ends of gear.

The do-it-yourself instinct in the outdoor group really has deeper roots, however, than necessity, logic, and fiscal reality. It is an extension of our collective desire to be independent of society. Just as we get an enormous feeling of accomplishment by spending a week or two in the farthest reaches of the wilderness, we also feel great satisfaction in using tools, shelters, equipment, and gadgets made with our own hands. Besides, it is a good feeling to know we can do it without the million-dollar efficiency of modern industry.

Of course, beyond these deep-seated theories that justify our involvement with saws and hammers and needles and thread, the average backpacker makes at least part of his own equipment for another reason—it's jolly good fun! To take a cast-off peanut tin, a bent-up clothes hanger, and a little solder, and then produce a rational, usable device is a special joy that keeps all of us busy looking for new fields to conquer (and keeps the nation's hardware stores solvent).

The reasons for getting knee-deep in the do-it-yourself action are, as we have seen, numerous, and the effects of this activity are even more widespread. By making a piece of equipment that is not normally used (or available) in a certain area, we can greatly expand our outdoor options. Many activities are, for some obscure reason, limited to a geographic sector of the country, and only a few errant travelers or nomads would ever introduce one of them to another area. Thus, many of the projects in this book were chosen because of their geographic flexibility. The lowly crawfish, for example, is abundant in practically every body of fresh or brackish water in North America, yet in only a few places are these delectable little shellfish seriously caught. In this book, there are two different traps that will allow virtually anyone—anywhere — to explore and enjoy the succulent delights of a crawfish cuisine.

Another typical example of a regionally limited device included here is the gaiter, a lightweight protection against soggy pant legs and gravel in the boots. Almost a standard fixture among the high-elevation hikers of the Northwest and the Rockies, this simple garment can be a boon to hikers in *any* section of the country.

A few of these projects were first illustrated in magazine articles and the response was so enthusiastic that the idea for this book was born. All have evolved from the ideas of several experienced outdoor people and many are variations of some pretty old themes that have not been successfully duplicated by the mass production manufacturers. None of these designs is overwhelmingly difficult—as long as a person has an average number of thumbs, that is. True, some require basic skill at the sewing machine, and a few require a slight talent for using hand tools, but nothing in here demands journeyman-level skills. With a little time and patience, the most helpless among us can satisfactorily complete any project in this book.

Finally, each project has been used by one of a handful of friends, usually with complete success. Even when things *didn't* go as planned, it wasn't the project that failed; I mean, it wasn't my fault that ol' Duane Watkins lost his knife from the loss-proof sheath. He also lost the sheath, his pants, and a three-day supply of groceries when he steered his canoe into a particularly obnoxious rock!

All things considered, the projects should give the builder a sense of accomplishment in the building, and a greater feeling of self-sufficiency when the finished projects are used in the field. They were selected on the basis of ease of construction, usefulness of application, and pure, unadulterated fun. We certainly hope it works out that way for everyone who tries them.

Tricks and Tools

Most of the projects in this book are of the simplest nature and are easy to complete. Still, the broad spectrum of outdoor enthusiasts ranges from those who can breeze through a cornea transplant to those who have moderate difficulty plucking a dandelion. We hope the instructions are complete enough for the latter without dreadfully boring the former. In many cases the project is flexible enough to keep everybody interested; it can be as primitive or as polished as the skills of the builder.

To be fair to those who find a soldering gun or a sewing machine a hopelessly involved device, we should take a brief look at the tools and techniques that will be encountered along the way. As with most of life's little mysteries, a quick discussion of the fundamentals does a lot to draw back the veil of darkness.

Hammers and Nails

Perhaps the simplest construction practice in the projects (one that is intimately familiar to anyone who has ever owned, rented, or lived in a house) is joining two pieces of wood with a nail. About the only problems that can come up are either (a) hitting something other than the intended nail, or (b) splitting the piece of wood. The obvious solution for the first is to improve your aim. The second problem occurs if you use too large a nail and accidentally split a chunk of laboriously cut

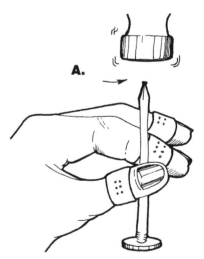

A. Gently tap the nail to dull it. You can then drive it in without splitting the wood.

and frightfully expensive wood. Often, it happens because the nail pushes the wood grains apart, causing the whole to separate. This problem can be overcome (seriously!) by simply dulling the end of the nail. Just tap the sharp end of the nail with the hammer as shown and the blunted end will break the wood fiber rather than forcing itself between the grains. In nearly every case, this trick creates a firm, tight joint without splitting the wood.

Soldering

This is one of the easiest ways to join two metals without the aid of expensive welding equipment or mechanical connectors. The joint produced is suitable for only very light metals and wires, but there are several projects that incorporate this technique. One difficulty of a soldered joint, however, is the low heat needed to remelt the solder. If a backpack grill were soldered (as opposed to welded), the heat from the campfire would reduce the device to a pile of disconnected wire rubble!

The proper method of soldering, with either a "gun" or an old-fashioned iron, is to heat the material to be soldered, allowing the collected heat to melt the solder. Joints constructed by simply melting the solder over the proposed joint are seldom strong enough to be trusted. In many cases, the joint can be mechanically strengthened by twisting the wires or rods *before* applying the solder to the junction. The cascade drinking cup is a good example of both mechanical and soldered joints.

Sewing

Many useful and novel accessories are made of cloth. This means that every hiker and backpacker should eventually become a fairly skilled artisan with needle and thread. Some of the projects in this book require a number of essential seams in order to construct a top quality pack, tent, or other fabric accessory. It is, then, a good idea to become familiar with some of the basic stitches and seams that are needed. They are better illustrated than described, and the accompanying sketches should make the mystery a bit clearer to the uninitiated.

Plain Seam: This basic seam is a method for attaching two

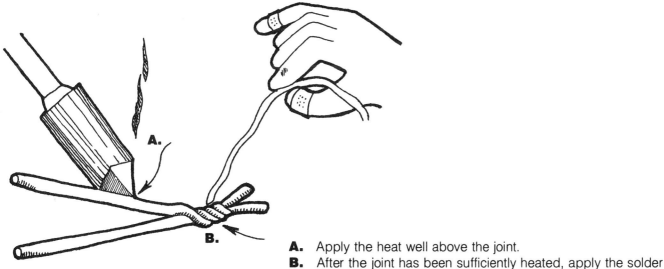

A. Apply the heat well above the joint.
B. After the joint has been sufficiently heated, apply the solder directly to the point to be connected.

pieces of cloth that generally lie in the same plane. There are many uses for the plain seam, which can be finished by binding and resewing with a binding of cloth tape. This seam is often used in making tents, flies, and gadget bags. If the basic fabric is nylon, the binding tape should also be a nylon weave because both pieces will tend to stretch equally. The illustration clearly explains this basic stitch.

Hem Seam: A variation of the plain seam, the hem is often used to finish a garment or gadget and provides a double thickness of cloth at the margins. This, of course, means the product is less liable to tear accidentally or fail during use. As with the former seam, this one can be either rough or finished, depending on the need and desire of the builder. A finished hem seam does not need any tape for binding; the base material is simply folded under itself, as shown.

Flat-Felled Seam: This is an important seam for joining large pieces of fabric (as in a tent or rain fly) or for making a water-resistant seam in packs, gaiters, and other exposed devices. Construct this seam by first sewing a rough plain seam, then folding both pieces to one side and sewing another course. You can finish the seam by folding the double thickness a second time, as shown in the illustration.

Top-Stitched Seam: This seam is designed to connect two layers of fabric at right angles to each other. Such difficult projects as sleeping bags, down-filled garments, and divided-room wall tents often require this seam. For our purposes, the top-stitched seam is restricted to such neat things as backpack pockets and storage-bag dividers. You make it (as illustrated) by sewing one fabric to the other at the designated point and turning the connected fabric up. Finish it by tucking the seam area under before sewing.

Insertion Seam: This seam is a rather specialized configuration that you usually use when joining a single layer of fabric to two or more other pieces. The backpack tent is a case in which you use the insertion seam to join only one layer of nylon to a single, heavier layer of the same material. (The insertion seam is illustrated on page 10.)

Metalworking

In a few cases, the projects call for some metal work because a series of small cuts and folds are necessary to make a movable joint. In these

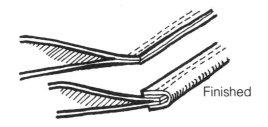

Plain seam

Finished

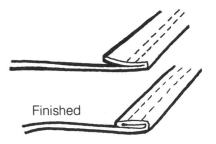

Finished

Hem seam

instances, the specific details are found within the illustrated instructions. None is too difficult, and if the task appears to be beyond your particular manual skills, you can probably farm it out to a local vocational school or metal shop for simple welding. The cost should be low, particularly if you have prepared the project first.

Materials

Few generalizations can be made about the vast array of materials that are used in the projects in this book. The specific material needs of each are discussed as they occur later, and those suggestions include (wherever applicable) substitutes that can be made with little or no reduction in the usefulness of the device.

The one constant in the selection of outdoor fabric is nylon; there is not a substitute of consequence for it in the backpacking arena. Specifically, most outdoor projects are made of a specialized nylon known as "rip-stop." It is a relatively sturdy fabric that is woven, depending on the grade, with every tenth or twentieth thread much heavier than the intervening ones. This results in a fabric that does not rip easily, resists damage, and weighs little in relation to its strength.

There are other nylon fabrics that are found in many manufactured outdoor items, including nylon pima and nylon taffeta, but these do not have the inherent strength of rip-stop.

Another benefit of using nylon for outdoor gear is that it is "breatheable" and prevents undue accumulation or condensation of moisture. This is an important factor in making tents, but it also allows greater comfort in many nylon garments and accessories.

In some design applications, the breatheability of nylon is a drawback; it allows rain to drip through, wetting whatever is inside. In the case of a backpack tent, the contents usually include the hikers! To combat this unfortunate property, two solutions have been devised. Either a separate, waterproof cover is provided for the tent, or the material is itself coated with a moisture-resistant compound. Although both methods of protecting the hiker against rain are fairly effective, both have their disadvantages. In the case of the rain fly (the better of the two choices), a significant weight is added to the backpacker's total load. The coated material, on the other hand, keeps the rain out

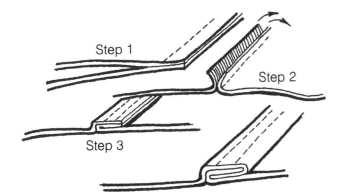

Flat-felled seam

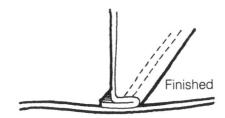

Top-stitched seam

with little added weight, but condensation inside the tent collects on the canopy and eventually drips on the occupants of the shelter. During very warm or humid periods, the collected condensation may almost equal a mild summer shower!

In recent years, experiments have been made to discover a fabric or coating that could protect the inside of a tent from moisture while still allowing the fabric to breathe. The breakthrough occurred recently with the development of an efficient material called Gore-Tex. It is not yet generally available to the do-it-yourself craftsman, but we hope it will be—and soon!

It is possible to construct some smaller fabric designs in the project list using a material other than nylon. In the case of the stripping basket, the canvas creel, or the rock sample bag, it is usually wise to choose a good grade of waterproof canvas. The heavier material is almost immune to abrasion, can take rough treatment, and the finished item is too small for you to worry about its weight. There are literally hundreds of grades and types of cotton canvas that you can purchase in a yardage or awning shop.

The tools and materials used in these projects are almost as flexible as the designs themselves. Although we will recommend a specific product to serve the purpose, you can usually find a substitute, often from whatever is on hand. For instance, if the design and instructions call for a piece of leather, as in the case of the fly book, it is not necessary to go out and *buy* a chunk for that purpose if an old cast-off purse is just collecting dust in Aunt Ida's closet. Sometimes a little conscientious scrounging around the neighborhood and prowling about the local thrift shops will turn up exactly what you need—at a fraction of the cost of a new material.

After all, if we can get the material for free, invest nothing but our own enthusiasm and effort, and still get the comfort and convenience of an enlarged gear inventory, isn't that what it's all about? And if we expand the quality of our experiences in the process, we will all be a little richer for it!

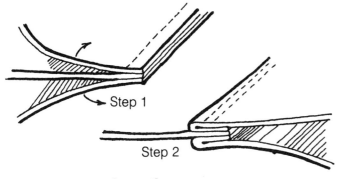

Step 1

Step 2

Insertion seam

The Projects

The projects on the following pages will keep your do-it-yourself instinct alive and well while you dwell in your workshop or at your kitchen table.

None of the projects takes a lot of material (except, perhaps, the backpack tent and associated rain fly) or many highly specialized tools and equipment. You may need to have some basic welding work done or borrow a sewing machine, but a little bartering or some good old-fashioned salesmanship will keep the cost low and the needed tools within reach.

In any case, when a certain project appeals to you, you will find a way to make it all work. If you were not that kind of person, you probably would not have bought or borrowed this book in the first place!

Cascade Cup

One of the most romantic pioneer scenes of contemporary movies and television features a grizzled old frontiersman of yesteryear leading his equally grizzled mule through a soft and lovely meadow. The mule invariably bears a couple of large, canvas-wrapped boxes from which swing all the tools and trappings of that solitary and desirable kind of life. Most evident and unchanging are the pots and pans that bring to mind the pungent smells of woodsmoke and fresh-boiled coffee, and the quiet meals that they accompanied. And, of course, the movies have this all surrounded by a Technicolor sunset.

The whole picture might not have been so comfortable or romantic as all that. The old prospector was probably chronically hungry and cold, and his mule undoubtedly suffered the ravages of ticks and sore feet. But the modern hiker apparently feels a curious kinship with his ancestor of that bygone era. A weird assortment of gear swings and clangs on multitudes of packs along almost every hiking trail in the country.

The most universal of these gadgets and geegaws is a drinking cup. In practice, having a cup outside the pack is a good idea. At a rest stop, you can simply unhook it, have a drink, and hang it back on your pack — without the bother of opening and repacking the load. One of the neatest cups is this cascade cup, which is made of nothing more than a peanut tin and an old clothes hanger.

To make this project, it is important to choose a *peanut* tin rather than one that originally contained soup, corn, or anything else. There are

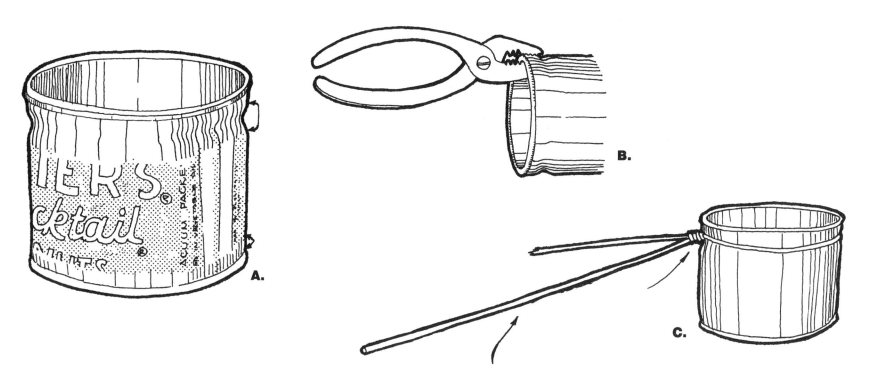

A.

B.

C.

three essential reasons for this choice. First, a deep channel encircles the top of the peanut tin and will hold the upper handle support for the cup. Second, the tin comes with a fitted plastic lid, which is important for carrying a tea bag or soft drink mix *with* the cup. Third, and most important, the peanut can has an alloy rim (bonded to the tinned steel body) that cools fairly rapidly when heated liquid is inside the cup.

In practice, the light metal (compared to commercially made cups) requires less than half the heat needed to boil water — an important consideration to the backpacker who must carry his own fuel. The vertical shape of the cup, again compared to the rather flat commercial cup, keeps the liquid warm longer. Finally, the junction of the handle and the cup acts as a thermocouple, drawing heat away from the upper part of the cup so you can drink the liquid comfortably.

The cascade cup is not so sturdy as a commercial cup, so it will eventually corrode on the outside or even weaken through repeated heating. But what the heck — it will last a couple of seasons at least, and it doesn't cost a cent to make a new one!

A. Sandpaper the paint from the upper groove so that the thermocouple effect will work, and ½ in. above the bottom rim of the tin so that a clean, fast solder joint can be made.
B. Crimp the edge of the upper rim carefully to remove any sharp edges or burrs that may cut the lips. Do not remove the upper alloy rim.
C. Using wire from a clothes hanger, cut a 25-in. piece for the handles. Wrap it around and twist the joint.
D. Form the square handle grip, and bend it around the bottom of the tin to make a snug fit.
E. Solder a joint. Heat the tin and wire before applying solder.

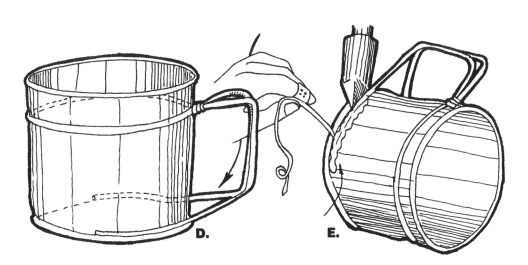

Backpack Oven

There are few outdoor arts that have progressed as rapidly as the business of eating. In the past few decades, we have gone from a bacon-and-beans fare cooked in a cast-iron skillet to such delicacies as turkey tetrazzini fixed in the backpacker's equivalent of a french oven. After a rather short evolutionary period, we have been blessed with every imaginable version of dehydrated, freeze-dried, enriched, and vacuum-packed food. And most require nothing more than a warm breeze to complete the cooking and serving processes.

Although the outdoor gourmet's hardware has also improved, mainly through the development of newer and lighter metals, we are still accustomed to sadly dismissing certain treats as patently out of reach — such culinary delights as fluffy cakes, cinnamon rolls, and the Yankee pot roast.

But these delectables — and an unending list of others — are suddenly within the realm of possibility! The device that will satisfy our innermost mealtime lusts is the simple backpack oven. To add one to your backpacking essentials, begin by dropping by the nearest hardware store or thrift shop and securing a ten-inch angel food cake tin

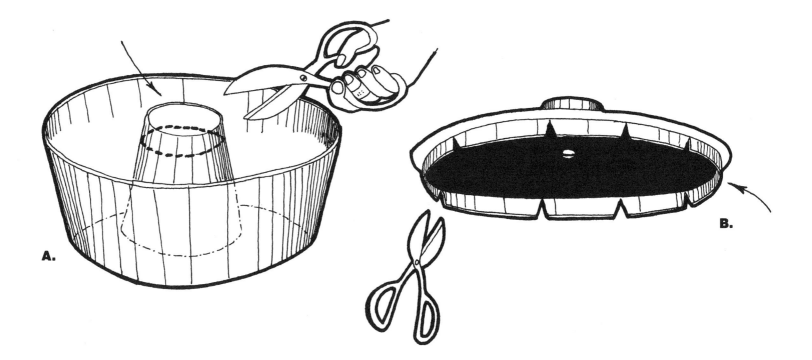

A.

B.

and a lid that fits it. Because of the steep, tapered sides of the pan, you may be forced to adapt a cover that *almost fits*.

Once constructed and then placed over a little backpack stove, this pan and lid will be transformed into an oven capable of baking biscuits, roasts, or angel food cakes. (It is even possible not to burn the bottom of an angel food cake!) This oven adds an entirely new dimension to camp cookery, and weighs just a tad compared to the benefit it provides. Moreover, it can be assembled in short order for about one tenth the cost of a comparable commercial model.

A. Make the oven body out of a 10-in. angel food cake tin. Using wire cutters, cut off about 1 in. from the top of the inside center column.

B. Fit a 10-in. cookware lid to the oven body, being careful not to wedge the lid in too tight. At about 2-in. intervals, cut a series of V notches. Tabs will be formed at the same time.

C. Bend the tabs inward until the lid conforms to the angled sides of the cake tin. The form-fitted cover should fit snugly.

D. When using your backpack stove, keep it on low heat, allowing the dry heat to draft up the center column. This also helps to keep the bottom of the pan from burning.

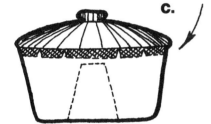

Reflector Oven

There is perhaps no single device in the backpack inventory that has been viewed with quite so much suspicion and disbelief as the reflector oven. To a hiker who associates open fire cookery with half-burned-and-half-raw food, ash and grit in the oatmeal, and lightly smoked eggs, the thought that a metal abomination can actually bake biscuits is akin to outright quackery! Yet a great many people have prepared countless meals with the aid of a reflector oven, and have done the job nicely. My father started his outdoor career as a camp cook, and he was sometimes known to cook for a hungry survey crew by using nothing more than a tin can, a green-maple twig, and a reflector oven. With these simple tools — and a handful of anonymous ingredients — he could still

their rumbling stomachs, if not their derisive hoots and catcalls!

In principle, the reflector oven combines direct and reflected heat to provide an almost perfectly even heat on the cooking shelf. With practice and the proper fire (long lasting, hot coals are the best source of heat), it works exactly as it is intended to. The modern hiker who has learned to control his fire and correctly use this wonderful utensil is looked on by his contemporaries as a sort of magician — and he sometimes is!

The oven is made from a few square feet of aluminum or wafer-thin steel, and is easy to make if you have only a little experience in metalworking. (A more accomplished metalworker may vary the design in order to make it lighter or easier to fold.) More important than the actual design (to the backpacker anyway) is the light weight of the oven, so aluminum is usually used. It also will not rust.

Even though the reflector oven may take a little patience to assem-

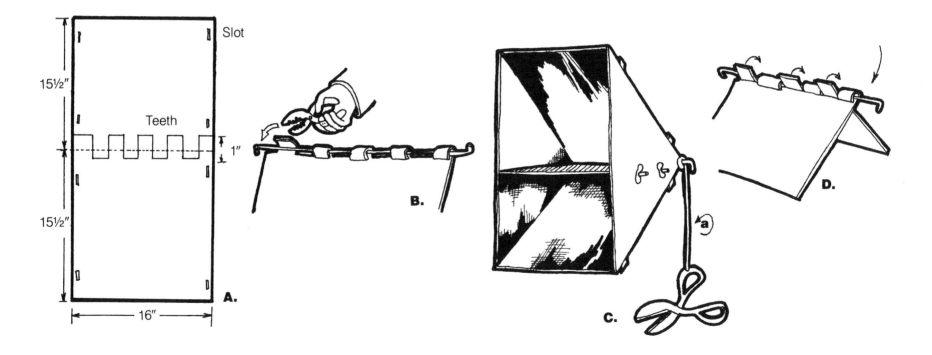

ble and a little practice to use, it may well become one of the most valuable cooking utensils in your pack.

A. To make the back reflector, cut a 31-in. piece of sheet metal stock into the dimensions shown, making sure that you cut out the "teeth" so that they interlock. Then cut 8 slots, 4 on each side of the sheet. These will connect to the side panels of the oven.

B. Make the hinge by bending the metal tabs of 1 piece of the toothed sheet metal around an 18-in. piece of clothes hanger wire. Let 1 in. of wire extend past each side.

C. Bend two 18-in. pieces of wire around these two 1-in. pieces (a). These longer support wires can be pushed into the ground and will keep the oven at a proper angle to the fire.

D. Complete the hinge by inserting the second sheet tabs and bending, as illustrated. The back reflectors will now fold into an easy-to-carry 16 × 15½-in. package.

E. Cut the 2 oven side panels to the sizes shown. Leave 4 tabs on each side panel to fit into the slots on the back reflectors. Drill 2 holes on each side, to which the cooking shelf will be connected.

F. Cut the cooking shelf to size. Rivet four 8-24 eyebolts in place, as shown, being sure to line them up with the holes in the side panels. This nut and bolt system holds the entire oven together.

G. Note that the shelf is about ½ in. narrower than the reflector back. This differential allows the sides to be joined tightly with the eyebolt and wing nut connectors. Once you have the side panels connected to the reflector back and the cooking shelf screwed in place, you are ready to cook.

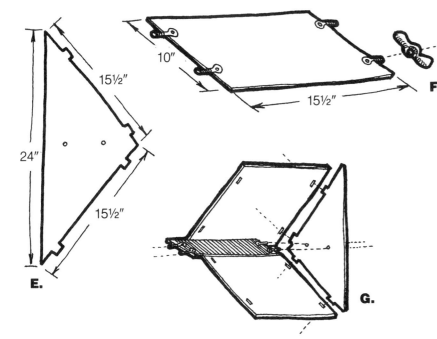

Backpack Grill

The backpack grill is a piece of equipment that is often overlooked by hikers. The grill, when suspended between two stones in the fire pit, can allow several dishes to be cooked at the same time and provide a place to keep coffee and other items warm — and it does it all with little confusion or effort. This grill is easy to make, light to carry, and an invaluable accessory.

Quite different, however, is the question of *when* the grill should be used. A few years ago, the campfire was considered as much a part of the outdoor scene as the rain, the hills, or the sunrise. It was a fact of life that was taken for granted — unless a heavy rain came along! But today, because of a combination of factors — the prime one being the growing number of people using the wilderness areas — the right to build a fire is no longer an unquestioned assumption.

When you are in an outdoor situation that lends itself to open fire cooking, try the simple backpack grill shown here. It is bent from a piece of heavy stainless steel tubing. You will have to have minor welding

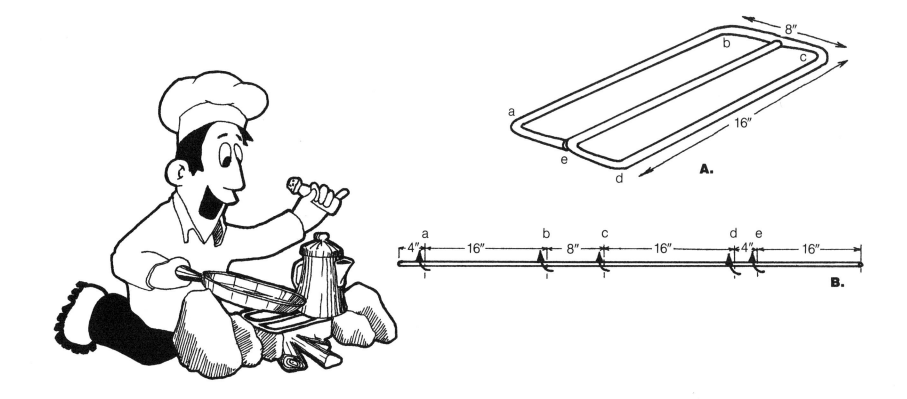

done, but the result is worth far more than the nominal fee.

The carrying bag is almost as important to comfort and efficient operation as is the grill itself because it keeps all the other gear inside the pack from getting a thick coating of soot when the grill is stowed. Make it out of lightweight nylon, and if you have trouble making it, refer to the nylon utility bag project.

A. Make the backpack grill from a single piece of stainless steel tubing. Use ⅜-in. to ½-in. heavy wall tubing.

B. Bend the tubing according to the dimensions shown. If possible,

bend it on about a 1-in. radius.

C. Have the grill welded in order to prevent its warping after repeated exposures to fires.

D. Cut a piece of nylon to the dimensions shown. Hem in a drawstring at the top. Turn the material wrong side out, and sew up the bottom and 2 side seams. Turn the bag right side out and insert the finished grill.

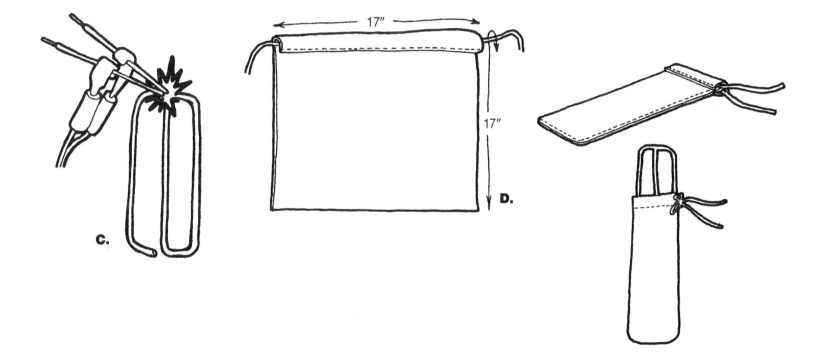

Hobo Stove

There is a certain charm about using a primitive, traditional piece of equipment in the field. I do not know whether we are progressing by turning back to such a tradition, or if we are regressing to a simpler age, but all of us seem to enjoy trying one of the old gadgets, especially if the thing works.

The hobo stove traces its ancestry clear back to the invention of the number ten tin can. It became prominent during America's Great Depression following the crash of 1929. This economic tragedy thrust a great many people into the unfamiliar role of vagabond — they learned to take advantage of whatever resource appeared. The number ten tin was a product of the period of relative affluence that immediately preceded the crash, and it was seized by the *nouveau bum* community as a staple of survival. The tin served as stove, water carrier, serving dish, suitcase, and sole eating container for an enormous migrating society. As such, it became one of America's most cherished resources.

The stove that was fashioned by these knights of the open road was ingenious, efficient, and practical. It has lost none of these qualities today. For the low-budget backpacker, it offers the added advantages of being lightweight, simple to operate wherever fire is allowed, and practical because cooking utensils can be nested inside.

Because of its construction, the stove retains heat longer, distributes heat more evenly across the upper surface, and prevents rapid

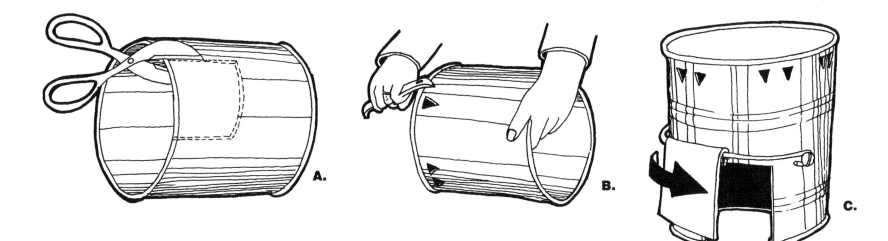

A.

B.

C.

burnout of the can, which otherwise could occur. Remember to use only pencil-size bits of wood for the fire under the stove. Since the fire is almost entirely contained within the tin, the amount of heat generated and transferred to the cooking surface is enormous. By using the damper, you can also control the intensity of the fire inside.

Even though the pain of the Depression has been diminished by the passing of generations, none of us would care to return to those difficult days. Rather, we prefer to borrow from the ingenuity that conquered the Depression and enjoy the hobo stove, an interesting artifact from the past — and an efficient cooking system for the present.

A. Remove the lid from the bottom of a #10 tin can and cut a 4-in. square door along the lower margin of the tin.

B. Place the removed bottom lid inside the top of the tin; punch several smoke holes with a can opener in the top of the tin. The can opener tabs will keep the second lid inside so it can act as a durable double top.

C. Just above and to 1 side of the 4-in. square door, drill a hole. Insert a bolt in the hole and secure it on the inside with a nut. Repeat on the other side of the door. Attach either end of a wire to each bolt. (Soldering does not work as it may melt because of the inside heat.) Take the 4-in. square you removed from the tin and bend it over the wire as shown. Open and close the damper, as needed, to control the intensity of the fire.

D. Hobo stove in use

Backpack Rod Carrier

Getting the fishing gear to the mountain intact can be just as challenging to the high-country or backpack fisherman as catching fish. Because of the rigors of low-hanging brush, slippery trails, and unexpected limbs, altogether too many excellent fly and casting rods reach the lakeshores in totally unserviceable condition. It is true that some short fishing rods have been developed specifically for the hiker, but many dedicated anglers refuse to part with the action and control of a long two-piece rod.

There are several ways to protect that precious fly rod while on the way through the hinterlands, and perhaps the easiest of these is to go out and *buy* a commercially made aluminum or plastic case. An alter-native is to make one at home that is every bit as light and rigid, yet costs only a fraction of what we pay for a ready-made.

The choice of material depends on what is available in a given locale and what medium you prefer to use. Whether you choose spun aluminum, lucite tubing, or PVC pipe (all of which should be available in a hardware or plumbing supply store), the technique is essentially the same. The main consideration is the desired combination of light weight and rigid protection.

Of the available materials, PVC pipe seems to be the best bet. It is available in every town and hamlet, can be bought in a wide variety of sizes and thicknesses, and costs far less than most of the alternate materials.

Choose a piece of pipe about two inches longer than the longest section of the rod you carry. The diameter of the pipe, of course,

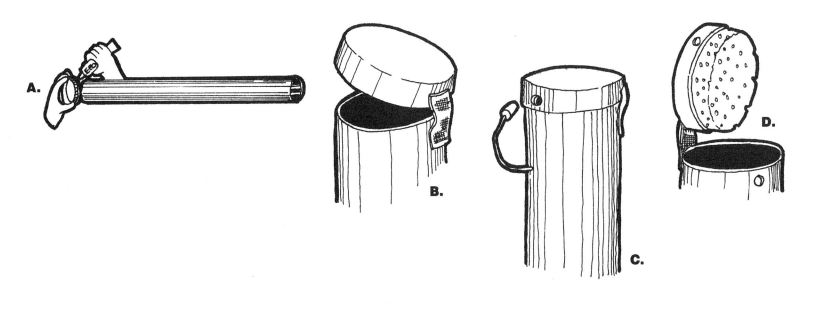

depends on the size of the rod and handle; the thickness depends on what is available and how much protection your rod needs.

In addition to the pipe, purchase *two* PVC caps to fit the ends of the pipe, a small tube of epoxy cement, and (if you can't scrounge some) about eight square inches of inch-thick foam rubber or polyethylene foam.

Now you are ready to make the carrier. The simplicity of this device is no deception. It is easy to make, requires absolutely no maintenance, and keeps the precious fishing rod in top shape on the roughest of backpack treks.

A. Cut the pipe or PVC tube to a length that is 2 in. longer than the rod. Take the bottom cap (made from a PVC cap) and pad its inside with rubber or polyethylene foam. Secure the cap to the bottom of the rod

with strong epoxy cement.

B. Make a hinge for the removable top cap by cutting a 1-in. piece of nylon webbing and cementing it to the top cap and tube as shown.

C. Drill the top cap and tube so that a wooden or plastic plug can be inserted in the holes to secure the cap. To prevent losing the plug, connect the cord to the tube with epoxy glue.

D. Cement a foam pad inside the top cap.

E. Use epoxy to glue on 2 carrying straps of nylon web with all-purpose buckles.

F. Completed rod carrier

Classic Fly Book

As it keeps flies clean, handy, and in proper condition, a fly book is an essential when challenging the wily trout. The classic book — usually stuffed with tattered remnants of bygone fishing trips, fond memories, and a marvelous assortment of artificial angling lures — is almost a relic in modern times. Unfortunately, most fisherfolk have replaced such fare with plastic boxes and brightly colored geegaws. The person who decides to use a fine old fly book on a trout stream is at least respectful of a bygone era, if not a stubborn traditionalist.

The book is made up of a folded leather cover that is lined with sheared fleece and closed with either a zipper or snaps, although the oldest ones were kept closed with a buckle or a tied bit of cotton tape (we yield to the modern efficiency of zippers or snaps here!). The dimensions given are merely guidelines because many anglers have a firm preference for the size of their books. The final dimensions can vary greatly, depending on the kind of flies carried, the size of your pockets, and just what feels right.

The outer cover of the book is usually made of real or synthetic leather. Although leather is expensive in comparison with almost any synthetic or fabric you can buy, it is also better, and can be salvaged from an old or cast-off purse in order to limit your expenses. If you use a

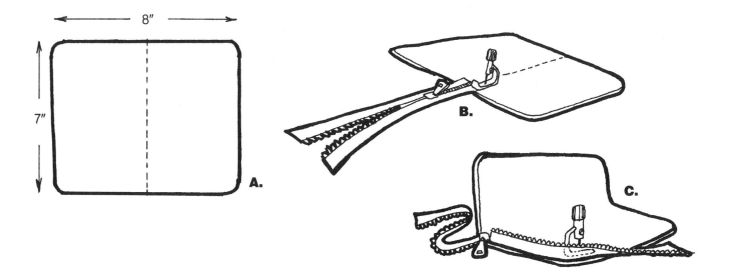

sewing machine, remember that leather is tougher than an equivalent thickness of cloth fabric, so a heavy-duty needle and thick dacron thread are appropriate.

The sheared fleece liner is nearly always made of an artificial material, primarily because real sheared fleece is either unavailable or exorbitantly priced. The artificial fleece works just as well and tends to shed water better. Some craftsmen sew the fleece in as the zipper is attached, but for most of us it is easier to cut and glue the fleece in after the zipper (or snaps) has been installed.

A. Make the cover by cutting a rectangle out of real or synthetic leather. The dimensions shown require a 14-in. zipper. For other sizes, make a paper pattern and determine the proper zipper size.

B. After separating the zipper, start sewing it at a perpendicular angle to the edge.

C. Fold the rectangle and sew the zipper all the way around the edges of the leather. When correctly sewn in place, the zipper will stand up all around, forming a shallow, boxlike book.

D. You can make a no-sew model by adding a fold-over flap (when you cut out the leather) and installing a snap. The ends remain open.

E. With either design, trim the sheared fleece and use contact cement to glue it in place after all other steps are complete.

F. Finished fly book

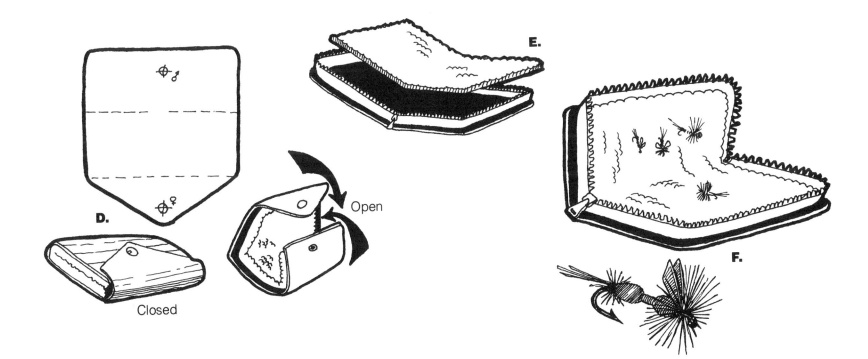

D.

Closed

Open

E.

F.

Fly Box

Because the typical fly-fisherman is endlessly intrigued by artificial flies, we are including one more container for these little gems. After all, some people have been known to collect *thousands* of flies in every conceivable pattern, size, color, and shape. It is doubtful that many of these flies will ever actually catch a fish, but owning a fine selection of flies is almost a requirement among veteran fisherpeople. We assume, of course, that the artificial fly looks enough like its natural counterpart to induce a clever trout to eat it. The trout undoubtedly thinks it is a gob of deer hair tied to a hook but, fortunately, trout will eat anything. My friend Zeke Watkins once caught a four-pound rainbow in Pearygin Lake (in Wash-

ington State) while trolling an heirloom butter knife. For several weeks, local anglers experimented with teaspoons, salad forks, gravy ladles, and even a perforated tea strainer. Most were successful!

The key to making this fly box is finding the right container. The best imported fly boxes are made of polished, anodized aluminum. (Some of the best are also covered with leather, but that embellishment was designed to catch fishermen, not fish.) All you need is a nice plastic or aluminum box. The sources of such containers, in a society that is enthralled with packages and boxes, are almost endless. My best fly box, incidentally, is a polished, spun-aluminum cosmetic case, which I "borrowed" from my daughter.

After you select a box, install the necessary holder that will keep the flies in good condition and readily available. One of the best arrangements for this is a low-tension coil spring. These coils look like miniature

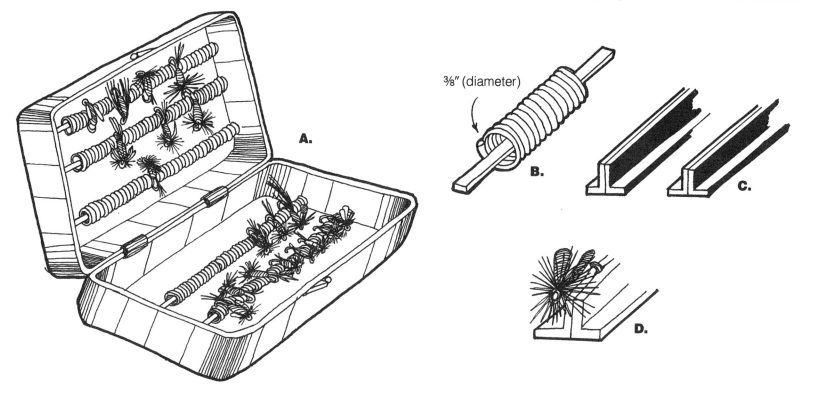

A.

⅜" (diameter)

B.

C.

D.

screen-door springs and can be purchased at many hardware, machine, and auto parts shops. The coil spring arrangement allows the box to carry more flies than the L beams (which are also shown), but either should carry all you need.

The nice thing about this project is that you can be as frugal or as sophisticated as you wish. I heard of one fellow who ordered a box of polished magnesium alloy, installed chrome-plated springs, and fitted the box with sixty-four hand-tied dry flies of various patterns, none larger than a #20! That, in fishing circles, is akin to Sainthood!

A. Make your fly box out of a plastic or aluminum box that is about 3 × 5 × 1 in.
B. Take several low tension coil springs, ⅜ in. wide and long enough to reach almost to the end of the box. Run a plastic or wood strip that is the same length as the box through each coil to the endwall of the box. Then glue the strips to the endwalls with epoxy.
C. You can make an alternate holding system with 2 L-shaped plastic channels. Glue the bottom of each channel to the bottom of the box.
D. The fly hooks go in the split between the unglued uprights, as shown.
E. Leave space between the springs of L-shaped holders so the individual flies are not crushed by one another.

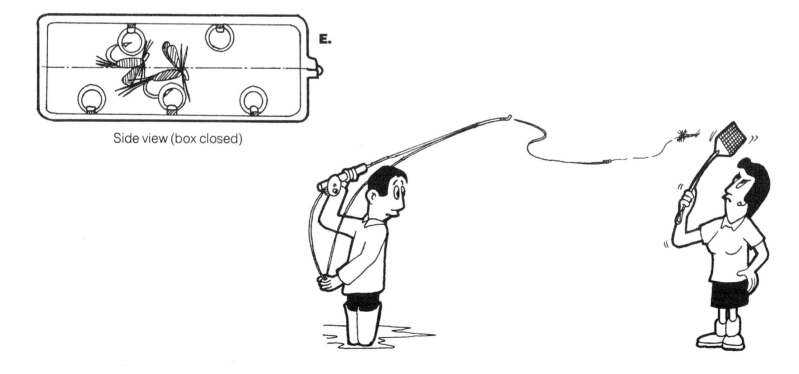

Side view (box closed)

Canvas Creel

Several hundred years ago, Izaak Walton decided to classify fishermen into several categories. He was profoundly unsuccessful, as anyone could have told him, because fishermen refuse to be categorized. They come in all sizes, shapes, persuasions, and income brackets. Seeing the vicar and the town drunk sharing the same stretch of water when the salmon are hitting is no more unusual than seeing a boy and his grandfather competing for the same bass.

But there is one thing all fishermen have in common — they are pushovers for the latest fads in lures, lines, rods, reels, and the rest of the gear that is spawned annually by manufacturers. This preoccupation with equipment has provided a wide open field for creel makers. You will find vests, wicker baskets, plastic boxes, leather pouches, gunny sacks, and almost anything else in which anglers can hoard their precious tackle. Understanding this, it is only appropriate that we have a creel in this book.

The canvas creel is made of a square canvas bag with a shoulder strap and several compartments in which you can store the aforementioned goodies. The major portion of the construction is on the front panel of the creel. (It would be possible to put pockets on the back side, but this would place the body of the angler and all those sharp hooks in immediate proximity, a situation that could lead only to trouble.) The upper compartment is a strip pocket that holds any manner of hooks,

A.

leader packets, small lures, and any other small paraphernalia. The design of the three lower, larger pockets depends partially on just how much gear you want to store in them.

Besides sparing you the cost of a store-bought creel, this canvas creel is simple to make and will confirm your status as an angler.

A. Cut the front panel out of canvas and hem it to the shown dimensions. Sew three 4 × 4-in. pockets to the front of the panel. Start with a 17½-in. piece and slowly gather it to make gathered pouches. Then stitch it vertically to divide it into compartments. Cut 3 cover flaps in one 12-in. piece of canvas. Sew this to the front of the creel above the pockets, as shown. Sew snaps onto the pockets so the pockets can be closed.

B. To make the 4 × 12-in. upper strip pocket, sew a strong piece of elastic tape to the inside of the strip. You can also sew real or imitation sheepskin, which can hold hooks securely, to the outside of the strip before sewing the strip to the bag. Sew 2 vertical lines of stitching to divide it into 3 compartments once it is attached to the bag.

C. Cut, hem, and sew the plain 10 × 13-in. back panel to the front panel. (Remember not to sew the top.) Add the shoulder strap (its length is determined by individual comfort) at the 2 joining places of the front and back panels.

D. The finished canvas creel

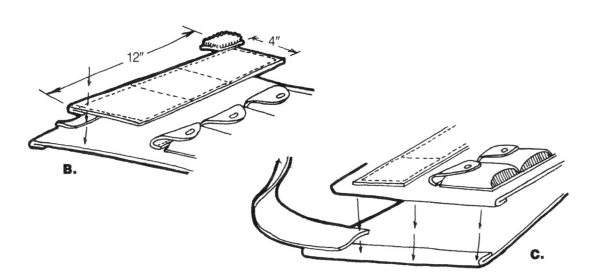

Stripping Basket

The stripping basket is an age-old fixture along many of the major fly streams of Europe, and has been around for a good many years in North America. The late Roderick Haig-Brown, probably the finest fly-fisherman of this century, was often seen fishing his favorite holes on Canada's Campbell River with his rod and stripping basket (and his labrador retriever). If it was good enough for *him,* it is certainly good enough for me!

The stripping basket is a receptacle that is strapped to an angler's middle; the basket receives the line as it comes in from a particularly long cast. It does not take a great fisherman to *use* a stripping basket, but it takes a darn good fisherman to *need* one! The basket becomes a decided advantage when the cast is longer than thirty yards, a rather common cast among the better steelhead and big-trout anglers.

The first model pictured here is a quick and easy rig to make. It is composed of an old thrift shop leather belt, a basket made of stiff canvas, and some duct tape, which holds it all together. Think of it — no sewing, no woodworking, no metalwork or soldering, and practically no cutting.

Once made, the basket is connected to the belt by cutting two belt loops along the upper back, as shown. The duct tape that holds the basket together is often used by heating and air conditioning contractors. It is a bit expensive, but there are a lot of jobs that it will do besides make a stripping basket, so go ahead and buy a roll. It sticks to practically anything, but if you feel that the bond is not quite strong

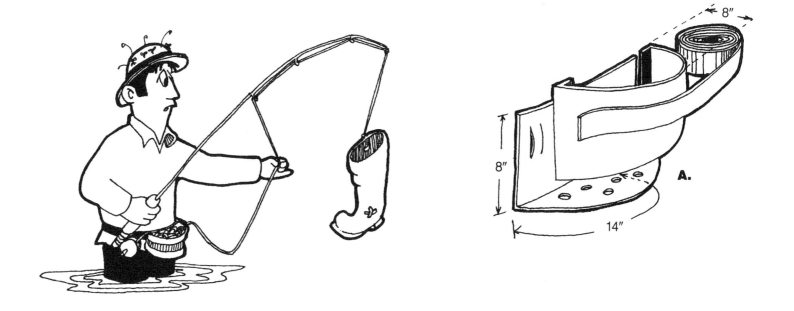

enough on the canvas, iron the aluminized back of the tape with a *barely warm* iron. Be sure not to get the "stickum" on the face of the iron — it is the devil to get off!

The second, more traditional stripping basket is made of hardware cloth. Just form a shallow basket, trim off all the excess little wires, and tape the top edge to prevent snagging. It works beautifully.

The stripping basket is a valuable device if you are a fly-fisherman. It keeps the excess line from getting tangled around your feet, keeps the line ready for the next cast, and makes you look as if you know what you are doing!

A. Following the above dimensions, cut the back and bottom of the basket from a single piece of "tin" (a heavy, stiff-weave) canvas. Cut the body from the same material and bend it to fit the curve of the bottom. You can cut several small holes through the bottom of the basket so water can drain from the basket. Use duct tape to hold the front and back/bottom together. If it does not stick, iron the back of the tape with a *barely warm* iron.

B. Connect the basket to an old belt by cutting 2 belt loops along the upper back, as shown.

C. You can make an alternate stripping basket out of hardware cloth. Cover the upper edges with duct or friction tape to prevent snagging a valuable fly line.

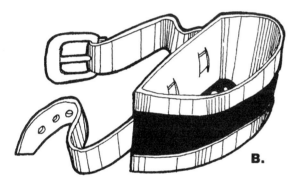

B.

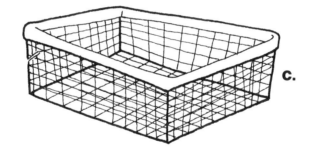

C.

Line Rack

We earlier made the point that the average fisherman considers accumulating equipment and gear (sometimes called "junk") a major part of his activity. In the early spring, usually about two weeks before fishing season opens, a primal urge begins stirring somewhere inside his winter fat. It ends only when he digs his trove of piscatorial paraphernalia out of the closet and starts "getting ready for the opener." It is an annual ritual that is practiced with the same devotion as a fertility rite!

The fisherman is not so much judged by his skill or catch record as by the amount and quality of his gear. If you see a kindly old codger whip a hand-tied muddler minnow from his patented English fly box, tie it to a 7X tapered tippet, and deftly cast it on the waters with his polished tonkin cane rod, you know darn well he is an expert. The fact that he has not caught a keeper trout since 1936 has absolutely no bearing on the matter; his deportment and gear signify that he is among the Chosen!

Actually, the condition of a fisherman's equipment is a lot better indication of skill than the price tag. If the equipment is clean and functional, you can pretty well bet the fish will follow. The best single element by which to judge an angler's skill is the fly line, probably the most overlooked of the major fishing components.

The fly line rack is the best accessory in the world for drying, storing, and dressing a good fly line. Most veteran fly anglers have such a rack, although some are no more than a large spool sitting on the closet shelf. This spool-type rack makes line removal and filling easy, keeps the line from adopting a permanent set, and stores several lines at one time. Our

sketch shows a spool of fairly narrow dimension, but it can handle three or four lines with ease. Many anglers prefer to make their spools about twelve inches wide, allowing plenty of drying and storage room.

A fine grade dry or wet fly line is a masterpiece of production. It is also appropriately expensive, so it makes good sense to keep it in top condition and ready for use at all times.

A. To make the spool ends, cut two 9-in. diameter discs out of ½-in. plywood. (They can be as large as 12 in. in diameter.) Mark 1 of the spools into 12 segments and locate the crossbar points about 1 in. in from the outside margins on each of the 12 lines.

B. On these marked crossbar points, drill the spools to accept a dozen ¼-in. dowels, and drill a ¼-in. axle crossbar in the center of the spool. Drill the 2 spools simultaneously to ensure proper alignment of the dowel holes.

C. Make the end supports out of ¾-in. wood and only slightly wider than the spool diameter. Drill an axle hole in the top of each end support so that each hole is a little larger than the axle crossbar; the spool should then rotate easily.

D. Nail the end supports to a flat board. Make the axle crossbar more than half the spool diameter in length and allow it to extend 4 in. beyond 1 side support so you can attach the handle crank to it. Glue the crossbar dowels in the spool ends.

E. Make the crank from a scrap of wood fitted with a dowel handle. Secure the crank on the handle with a small nail. To use, tie the line you want to store to 1 dowel and turn the crank. You can then easily transfer the line from the reel to the drying rack.

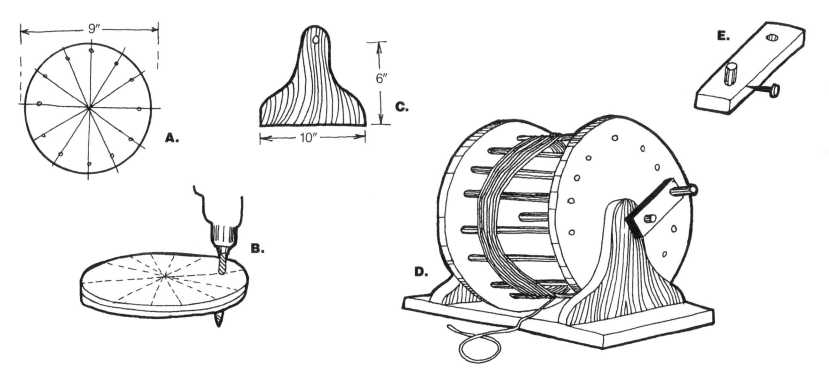

Fishing Travel Case

If you have been moderately observant while plowing through this book, you have gathered that I have succumbed to the lure of fishing. This is quite true, but the reason so many fishing projects are included in this volume is not so much to inflict the malady on others as to ease the symptoms of those who are already hooked. This fishing travel case is one of the best of the lot.

For years, I dragged my tackle around the country in cardboard boxes, smuggled it into hotel rooms in proper luggage, and otherwise tried to hide my affliction. I once even checked into a motel in Iowa (many miles from any decent trout water) with a very official-looking medical valise. I was treated with all due respect, but I am sure if the proprietor had known the bag contained an assortment of dry flies, hootchies, and bass lures, I would have been soundly thrashed and sent on my way. Then one day, after being unceremoniously tossed off a bus (just for practicing a few false casts down the aisle!), I decided to go legitimate. I built this marvelous tackle case, boldly labeled it "FISHING EQUIPMENT," and carried it right out in broad daylight. The effect was stunning. I am no longer bothered by crowds, I do not have to wait in long lines at the ticket counters, and the airlines no longer lose my luggage. It's a heady feeling, mate!

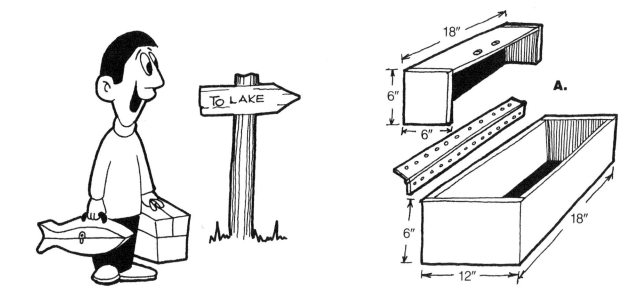

The travel case is constructed of half-inch plywood, built in the manner shown. You can line the upper flip-boxes with a thin layer of foam to protect your reels, but they actually do not have much chance of being damaged inside the case. You can easily carry three fly reels, two light spinning reels, and four assorted level-winds in the top and still have the entire bottom left for the other necessities.

The travel case can be varnished, or you may want to cover it with imitation leather or contact vinyl. Either way, it does not hurt to put your name and address on the inside — and outside — of the box for identification, and to label it as fishing equipment.

A. Make the travel case out of a base box and 2 upper flip-boxes.

Use ½-in. plywood. When closed, the box measures 12 × 12 × 18 in. Connect the 6 × 6 × 18-in. flip-boxes to the outside of the base box by using piano hinges, which are attached to the outside and require several screws.

B. Open the flip-boxes. Screw a 1-in. dowel along the bottom of each flip-box. Attach a few 1-in. thumbscrew hose clamps so you can securely clamp your whole reel inventory in place.

C. Install a hasp and lock on 1 end of the box. (You may also install a small sliding bolt on the other end if you will be carrying heavy loads.) Make 2 rope handles on the top of the box by running 2 short lengths of *knotted* rope through 2 pairs of holes in the top (closed position) of the box.

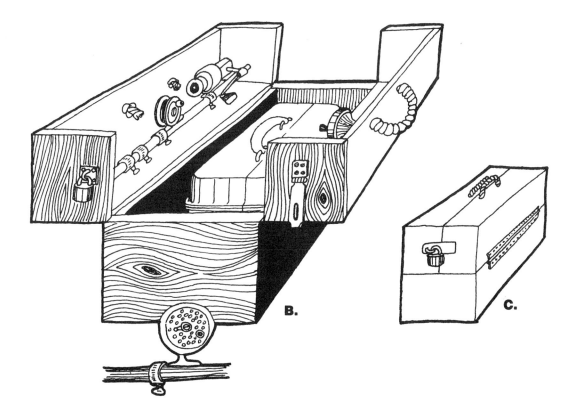

B.

C.

Fillet Board

When I first started filleting fish, I found that the simple procedure shown in the handbooks was anything but simple. Instead of whisking away a couple of perfect boneless fillets, I usually reduced the slippery little creatures to a state variously described as shredded asbestos, skinny scallops, or wet linen lace. If I did manage to carve a reasonable little fillet, it was either at the cost of around eighty percent of the original fish or several injured fingers, depending on whether I attempted frugality or safety.

One summer, in the midst of my frustration, I happened to go fishing with an almost retired commercial fisherman named Ed Brown. His mastery of filleting was exceeded only by his colorful vocabulary and legendary prowess at sea. In moments, Ed could transform a flopping, bucket-mouthed lingcod into a pile of the most beautiful, pure white fillets ever seen by man. The difference in his technique and mine (quite beyond the obvious difference between experience and novice enthusiasm) seemed to be only the board that firmly held his fish during the operation. In short order, I learned that a good filleting board was infinitely superior to holding the wriggling fish between my knees! In a relative thrice, I was filleting my fish with some degree of edibility if not outright artistry.

The fillet board consists of only a board and a clamp. The board serves as a platform that keeps the clamp — and subsequently the fish

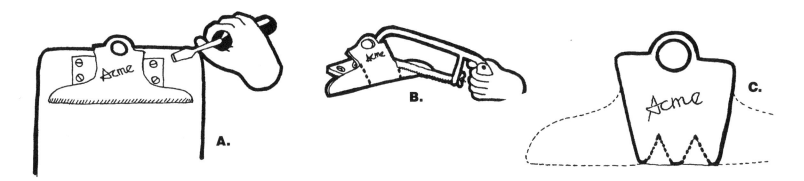

— in a stable position for dressing.

Since most of us are going to be filleting the occasional bass and rockfish that we land, the board need not be a large one. Oh, sure, if you are going to dress out a 400-pound sailfish or a record-class king salmon, you will need something more skookum. (You might try nailing the monster's head to the pier!) But most of us can get by nicely with about an inch thick, twenty-four-inch long fillet board. (The added weight of a fairly thick board helps keep your slippery quarry in the same county as you during the filleting operation.) *Do not paint or varnish the board.* It is better to occasionally replace the wooden part of your device than risk potentially dangerous paint chips in your dinner!

The clamp is a spring set of jaws that holds the beast in place while the dark deed is done. The standard office clipboard (with a good, strong spring) is ideal for fashioning into a nifty clamp.

This is another of those really simple devices that makes the whole outdoor business a lot more fun.

A. Remove the clip from a standard office supply clipboard.

B. With a hacksaw, remove the wide wings on either side.

C. Then saw notches into the face of the clip to create 3 or 4 teeth.

D. Bend the teeth into a slight downward curve in order to better secure the fish on the finishing board.

E. Mount the newly formed clamp onto a solid board about 12 × 24 in.

F. To use, just clip the fish onto the board, and use *both* hands to cut away the boneless fillets!

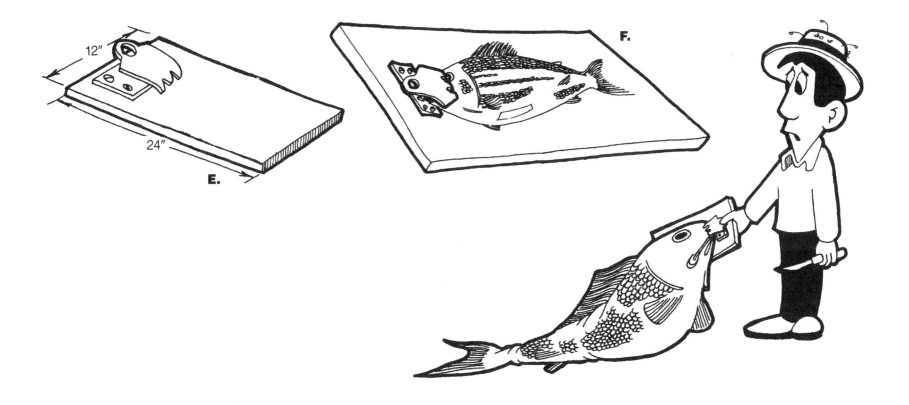

Crawfish Trap #1

As the name of this project may indicate, there is more than one way to skin a cat — or catch a crawdaddy! (The second, quite different trap is described in the next project.) This trap is a variation of one of the oldest fishing devices in North America, the New England lobster pot, and is constructed of four solid wood frames to which are nailed a number of laths, as shown in the accompanying diagram. The whole structure is covered with one-half-inch mesh net. Bait at the end of the tunnels on each end lures the crawfish in, and a door on one side enables the crawdad trapper to remove the bountiful catch. That's about all there is to making it.

As to using it — that's easy, too! The best bait is *not* — contrary to popular misconceptions — a chunk of well-seasoned fish. I have found crawfish to be pretty fussy eaters, and they greatly prefer a fresh fish to almost anything else. In an effort to be consistent and characteristically cheap, I usually bait my traps with a small tin of fish-flavored cat food. I punch a few holes in either end to let the wildly appealing odor (to a crawfish, at least) wash into the water to attract my quarry.

To make the trap sink — once you are ready to fish, that is — weight it down with a couple of hefty rocks or anything else that will make it sink. It is imperative, of course, that you tie a rope to the whole affair before you toss it overboard, unless you cherish the thought of swimming after it!

The weighted, baited trap can then be tossed into water practically anywhere, just as long as the water is relatively pollution-free. Crawfish live in almost every body of fresh or brackish water in North America, so keep looking until you find a hot spot. The trap is usually left overnight in order to catch the bigger crawfish, which are mainly nocturnal feeders.

When you bring in your catch, thoroughly rinse them, and then pop them into salted, boiling water for about five to seven minutes, after which they will be bright red and quite dead. Break off the tails, and peel

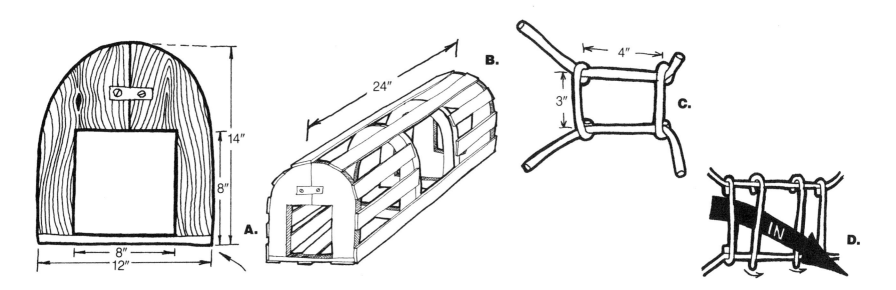

and devein them. Eat the 'dads as is or add them to almost any kind of seafood dish you like. Many people also eat the comparatively small but delicious bits of meat in the claws, a morsel that is usually referred to as "nectar" by crawfish devotees. It is a rare and delicate feast. When this lobster-type pot is so easy to build and use, it is incredible that the rewards from using it can include some of the finest seafood eating to be found anywhere.

A. This trap is made up of 4 wood frames: the frames at each end have *square* openings (which hold the 2 outside tunnels) and the 2 center frames have *curved* openings (see fig. F). Use 1 × 6-in. lumber for each frame. On each frame, saw the outside of each half into a curved shape, then connect each half with 2 screws and a piece of metal, as shown. Cut an 8 × 8-in. tunnel entrance out of the 2 end frames and cut the center out of each middle frame (see the proper shape in fig. F). Attach a 1 × 1-in. slat to the bottom of each frame.

B. Nail a number of wooden laths between the 2 ends of the 24-in. trap. Leave a side opening for the trap door.

C. Fit the 2 end openings with wire and net tunnel entrances. Make these 4-in. long entrances out of clothes hanger wire that is bent into a tapered *inside* opening of about 3 × 4 in. Solder 2 pieces of wire to the inner ends of the bent clothes hanger wire.

D. Bend 2 more wire "flaps," as shown, to prevent the prey from swimming *out* of the trap.

E. Cover the inside walls of the tunnel with ½-in. mesh net. Connect the bent tunnel to each end frame with 4 wood screws.

F. Build a door in the middle of the trap so you can remove your catch. Fasten a rubber strap to a few removable slats that are horizontal to the 2 middle wood frames. Use a wire hook and eye arrangement to keep the hatch closed while underwater. Old inner tube rubber and a home-fashioned hook and eye work well. Staple wire mesh over the trap door.

G. Cover the rest of the trap with ½-in. mesh net, as shown. Staple the mesh to the wooden laths.

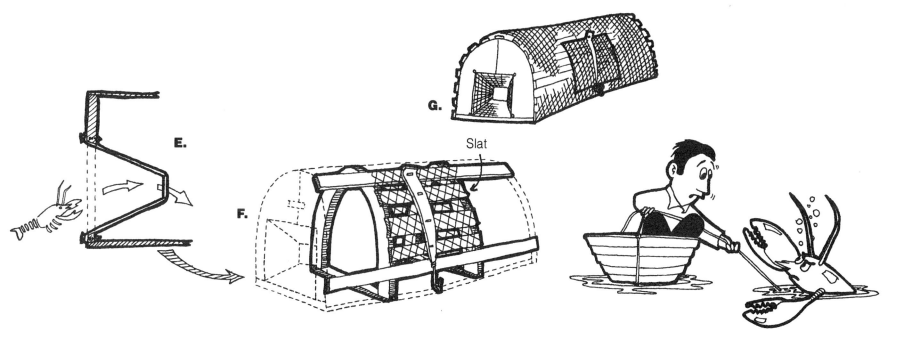

E.

F.

G.

Slat

Crawfish Trap #2

Actually, I have to thank ol' Duane for the general design of this next crawfish trap. The construction is a little different than the ones he made, but this particular trap is a lot easier to build. Despite the general similarity in appearance, Duane's trap was a real bear to put together. As I recall, he used about nine yards of sheet metal, the coil spring from a boxcar, and seven layers of overlapped chicken wire to get his built. I am sure it worked like a charm, but we were never able to find out for sure.

After he finally got it launched, it took three of us and Zeke Watkins's mule to get it back out of the lake. We never got to check it again — Zeke's mule died that same afternoon.

This second trap is different from the first in that it is cylindrical and constructed of hardware cloth, a rather folksy name for one-half-inch mesh galvanized wire. The hardware cloth can be purchased at almost any store bearing the same name and is relatively inexpensive. It is different from most other wires because, when you cut a piece of it with tin snips, little pieces of stiff wire protrude every half-inch along the fresh cut. These little wires are the means by which two pieces of hardware cloth are joined. Push the little wires through the solid wire on the edge of

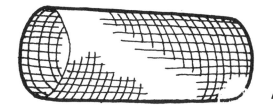

A.

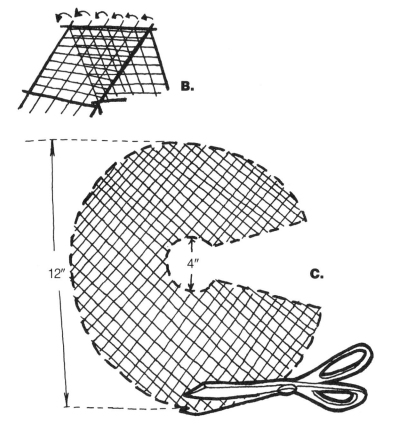

B.

12"

4"

C.

the other chunk of cloth (see illustration) and then bend them around the uncut wire like hinges.

When you complete this trap, bait and weight it as instructed for the first crawfish trap and you should have a crawfish feast in no time.

A. To make the body of the trap, take a 20 × 24-in. piece of hardware cloth and roll it into a cylinder. The diameter of the cylinder is 8 in.

B. Connect the ends of the hardware cloth where they meet on the cylinder by pushing the cut wires of 1 end through a complete course of wire squares on the other end. Fold the cut wires back onto the first end, as shown.

C. To make the tunnels, cut the cloth into a large circle (at least 12 in. in diameter for an 8-in. cylinder). Next cut a smaller inner circle about 4 in. in diameter.

D. Join the 2 sides of the tapered cut and you have a tunnel. Overlap the 2 edges to adjust for the proper size. Wire the tunnel closed and trim off all protruding wires. Wire the tunnel to the cylinder.

E. Cut a 6-in. square access door along the side of the tunnel. Connect the upper edge of the door to form a hinge using the same method as described in instruction B. You can fasten it with any wire hook or rubber arrangement.

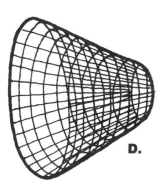

D.

E.

Clam Gun

Armed with a traditional hook-nosed shovel, many of us find the simple act of capturing a few succulent clams an ordeal. Yet it needn't be so! Thanks to a digger with a scientific mind, a length of irrigation pipe, and the immutable laws of pneumatic physics, we now have the modern clam gun.

The clam gun consists of a four-inch hollow tube and an interconnected tubular handle that act as a single airtight pneumatic unit. The aluminum irrigation pipe has given way to a thin-walled cylinder of stainless steel in many cases, but a few aluminum guns still exist. Either will do the job for most of us.

The gun requires two critical welded joints. Since the material in question is either stainless or aluminum, it would be best to send the welding to someone with the appropriate skills. The welding entails attaching the pipe upright to a disc that matches the gun's tube, and attaching the disc to the lower section. The rest of the device is fashioned at home from odds and ends of pipe.

To use the tube, insert it in the sand or mud over a clam (located by the hole or "show" it makes) and press down, leaving the thumbhole *open*. The air inside the tube escapes through the hole. When sufficient depth has been reached to capture the clam, close the thumbhole and

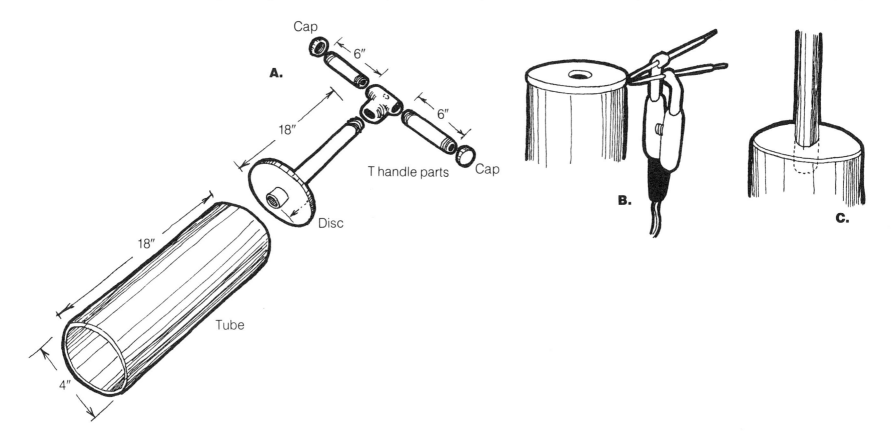

Cap

A.

6"

6"

18"

T handle parts

Cap

Disc

18"

Tube

4"

B.

C.

pull the tube up. Closing the thumbhole reestablishes the pneumatic vacuum and the gun comes up with the sand plug (ideally containing a clam) intact. After you release the vacuum, the plug will fall out onto the sand and you will find the quarry.

The gun is common on the hard-sand beaches of the Pacific, but you can use it with equal efficiency on most sand or mud beaches in North America. It has also been widely adopted for catching sandshrimp, a popular salmon and halibut bait.

A. The clam gun consists of a 4-in., thin-walled aluminum or stainless steel tube, a closing disc on top, and a galvanized pipe T handle, which is made of several pipe pieces. The caps on the T handle are essential for maintaining a single pneumatic unit.

B. Have the disc welded to the top of the tube.

C. Have the T handle welded to the disc. Allow the handle to extend about 2 in. into the tube for maximum strength.

D. Drill a ¼-in. hole in the T joint. This suction hole is critical to the operation of the gun.

E. To operate, push the tube down over the quarry. Leave the vacuum hole open on the downward stroke.

F. Seal the vacuum hole with your thumb on the upward pull, allowing the sand plug and the clam to be brought to the surface.

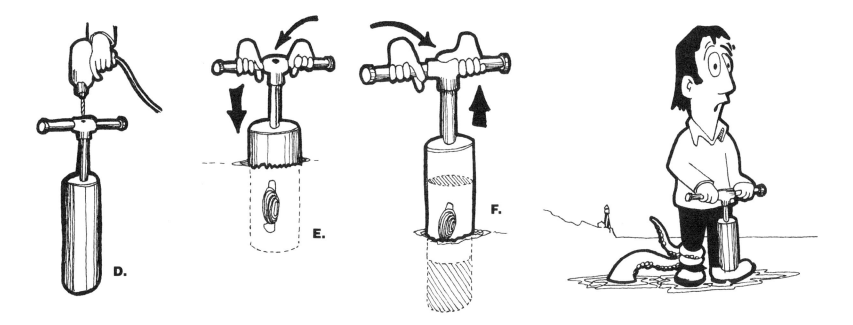

D.

E.

F.

Ring Net

One of the great joys of living near the ocean is catching your own supply of fresh seafood. Most of us do not live near the ocean, of course, but we can inexpensively, and without much training, gather a few delicacies on our infrequent trips to the coastline. Almost every bay, sound, and inlet (unless it is polluted beyond all hope) has at least one or two kinds of crustaceans that we can capture with a ring net.

The ring net is a marvel of simplicity, both to make and to use, and is not necessarily limited to salt water. Although there are two traps in this book specifically designed for catching freshwater crawfish, the ring net can take its fair share of these delightful morsels, too. So it is, as you can see, not at all limited.

The net is composed of two large metal rings, some fishing net between the two rings, and a rope with which to lower the trap to the bottom of the water. The upper ring is larger than the lower and thus forms a mesh bucket that is used to capture the quarry. Because the netting is laced onto the rings, the ring net forms a collapsible shape that lies flat on the ocean floor. (A big crab is easily caught in a three-inch mesh, but shrimp, prawns, and crawfish require netting no larger than one inch.) The bait is tied to the bottom of the net, where it soon attracts prey. (Use clams or fresh fish to attract shrimp or crab.) In shallow water,

you can see when something has entered the net, and you merely pull it up quickly. The combination of upward speed and the now-high sides keeps the shellfish inside the net until you get it aboard the dock or boat.

In deeper water you can only guess whether anything has entered the net, so pull it up every half hour or so until you determine how often the net should be tended. If there is an abundance of crab or shrimp, you may want to pull every five minutes. Unfortunately, the trapping isn't usually quite *that* good!

A. Make the ring net out of a bucket-shaped net and 2 heavy metal rings. Buy 1-in. mesh net at either a sporting goods store or cut it from stock net. For the 2 rings, use stiff (preferably copper) wire from either a scrap-metal yard or your local power company.

B. Make the rings any size, but be sure the lower is substantially smaller than the upper. (See drawing for suggested dimensions.)

C. Form the rings by hand. Bind them with several layers of soft, small wire. (Inspect them periodically for corrosion.)

D. Using sturdy nylon twine, which will not rot quickly, lace the net to both rings.

E. When you use the completed net, be sure to tie the bait to the bottom of the trap.

Crab Pot

So far we have looked at two crawfish traps and a ring net. You may think we are enthusiastic to the point of fanaticism about seafood — and you are right! There is a lot of good eating to be caught by the seafood fancier, a great deal of fun to be gained in the process, and a valuable lesson of self-reliance to be learned while it all happens. Now, if you happen to be what is charitably referred to as "thrifty," the money saved while indulging in such gourmet dining becomes a factor. If, like me, you are downright *cheap,* it becomes a *big* factor!

If you are serious about stocking the home larder with seafood, you will want to build a commerical-style crab pot. In most states, you are allowed to use at least one of these devices without a commercial license, but check the local laws before you toss one in the bay. Some states also require a small "escape ring" in the side of the trap so that small crabs can escape without being damaged. Ignoring such little details as marking buoys, fishing in legal areas, and using proper pots may land you in the pokey!

Make the pot out of steel tubing that is welded into a drum shape and covered with either fishing mesh or chicken wire. (The wire, incidentally, corrodes after about three days unless it is a special stainless steel mesh. The mesh is what the commercial crabbers use, but it is terribly expensive for us sport types. We can substitute nylon netting.) A tunnel opens a few inches above the floor of the trap at each end; once in, the crabs find it difficult to swim up to the elevated trap door in order to escape.

For baiting the trap, build a wooden box that has holes in it — the bait scent washes through the holes into the water and lures the crabs into the pot. Once trapped, the crabs cannot then leisurely devour the bait that is meant to attract many numbers of their kind. After filling with clams and fresh fish, suspend the bait box inside the pot by using surgical tubing and some wire hooks that you insert into the mesh.

Leave the pot in place for a day or two, but not much longer. If given sufficient time — three days or longer — the pot will "silt in," meaning

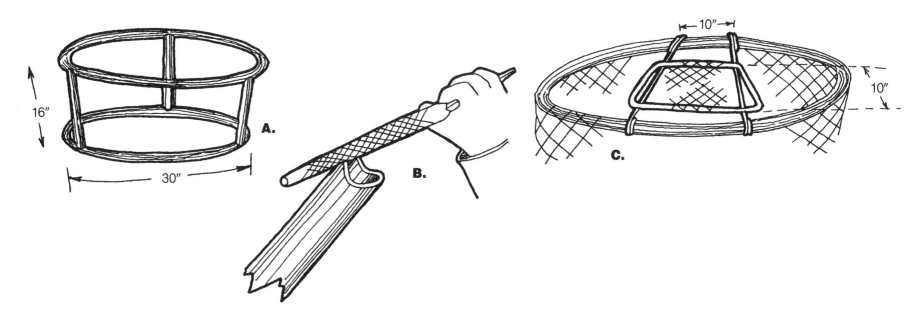

that it works itself into the sand. If it does silt in, you probably will not be able to retrieve it with anything less than a strong anchor winch. Check the pot every day or so — you should be rewarded with some pretty surprising catches (an added source of fun) and some true gourmet delights!

A. Secure 20 ft. of ¾-in. steel tubing to make the pot frame. Use a tube bender to shape the two 30-in. rings.

B. File three 16-in. uprights to fit the completed upper and lower rings. (Such preparation greatly reduces the cost of outside welding.) After the frame is completed, have it welded to the dimensions shown in fig. A. Coat the entire frame with a nontoxic latex paint after it is welded.

C. Cover the frame with 1-in.-mesh chicken wire or fishing net by wiring it to the steel tubing. Make a netted door in the top of the trap by cutting out a square of wire and then reinforcing the cut edges with a square of heavier wire. "Hinge" it by tying 1 edge to the mesh. Close it with a rubber-and-hook catch on the opposite edge.

D. On opposite sides of the pot, construct 2 tunnels out of stiff (preferably brass) wire. Make the tunnel's outer opening 8 × 12 in. and the inner opening 4 × 8 in. Solder the outer and inner rectangles to each other by using 4 pieces of connecting wire as shown. Once the tunnel is connected, the inner opening must be *at least 4 in. above* the trap's floor. (This makes entry easy and exit almost impossible for the crabs.) Cover the sides of the tunnel with stainless steel 1-in. wire mesh.

E. Cut through the trap's mesh covering to make an 8 × 12-in. opening for the tunnel. Run 2 sturdy pieces of wire vertically between the trap's upper and lower rings, as shown. Wire the completed tunnel to the vertical support wires.

F. Build a small 6 × 3 × 4-in. wood box with holes in it (for holding the bait). Latch the top closed, and install rubber hooks and straps to secure the box between 2 of the trap's edges so the bait hangs in the middle.

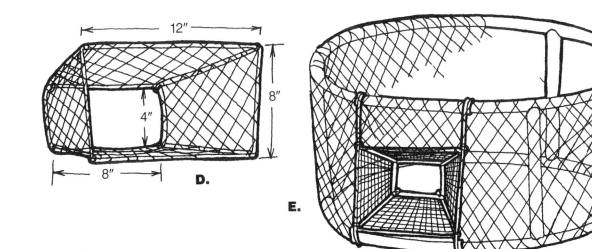

D.

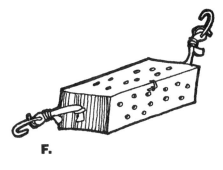

E.

F.

Alaskan Packboard

It seems only a few years ago that the famous Trapper Nelson pack or Alaskan board was the only kind of pack you would ever see in the woods. Before the advent of the aluminum-magnesium frame and the whisper-light nylon pack, it was the toughest, strongest, most practical rig to be found.

You would think that the coming of the lightweights would bring on the disappearance of the old boards, but they remain quite in evidence. In the miner's camp or the trophy hunter's bivouac, the Trapper Nelson pack is as important as ever, primarily because it helps the wearer carry a staggering load in relative comfort. Granted, it is no fun to wander

down the trail with 300 pounds of supplies strapped to the old-fashioned board, but it is a darned sight better than trying it with one of the modern tubular-frame packs!

You construct the pack's frame out of hardwood stock, the straps out of nylon webbing, and the cover portion out of heavy cotton canvas. When installing the straps, remember that the crossmembers eventually will be situated away from the wearer's back. When completed, the canvas cover will be stretched tight across the open part of the frame as a back support.

The Alaskan packboard may not be so sleek nor as comfortable as the modern frame pack, but if the load is large — or if tradition is your forte — it is the heavyweight classic of the wilderness trail. My father, incidentally, once packed a cast-iron stove into a lookout shack with one of these contraptions. Stalwart outdoor people have performed this feat

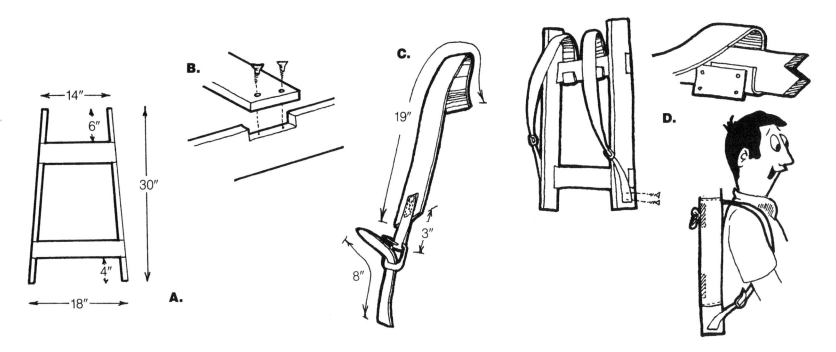

for generations, and it certainly illustrates the enormous capacity of this marvelous packboard.

A. Make the frame out of ¾-in. hardwood (¾ × 3-in. maple or ash is usually used); cut it to the dimensions shown.

B. Carefully fit both upper and lower crossmembers into the upright for a smooth, flush finish. It is a good idea to glue the joints carefully before setting the screws.

C. Make the straps out of 2½-in. nylon webbing cut to the shown dimensions. Sew leather straps (with a buckle) to the web so that the straps will be adjustable. You may also pad the shoulder straps for comfort.

D. Wrap the upper strap around the crossmember and secure it with a sheet of aluminum drilled for four ¾-in. screws. Remember that the crossmembers and lacing will be on the outside of the pack and the solid canvas directly against your back. (Wait to attach the bottom straps.)

E. Cut the back support out of heavy cotton canvas. Make sure it meets the shown dimensions after hemming all sides. Cut and hem an 8-in. hole in the upper center of the panel 3 in. below the hemmed upper edge. Install 7 grommets on each side, wrap the canvas around the frame, and close it with a 72-in. piece of nylon cord or rawhide.

F. The straps pass through the oval hole (seamed) in the back support. Connect the straps at the bottom with wood screws and fabric-support washers. Ask for these washers at the fabric store.

G. Screw eye screws into the laced side of the board. They will be used for lashing the load with cord or for attaching a custom packsack, which is our next project.

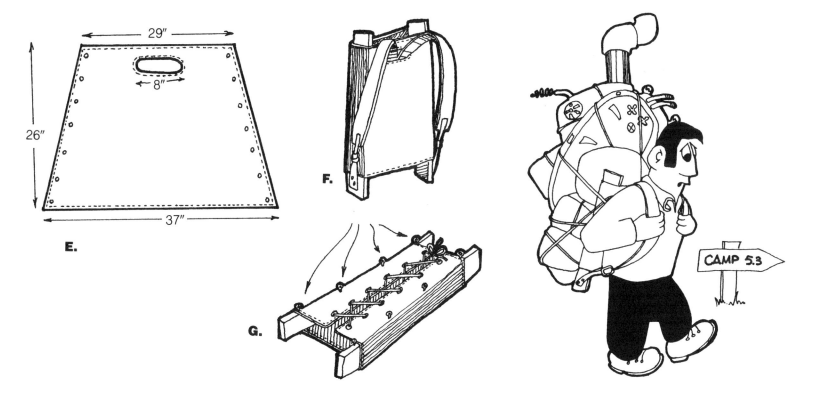

29″

8″

26″

37″

E.

F.

G.

CAMP 5.3

All-Purpose Packsack

A companion to the Alaskan packboard, this all-canvas sack is neither as light nor as stylish as the bright orange nylon creations of today, but like the board it is designed to fit, it is unbelievably practical. In the old days, it was not considered a bit unusual for a trail crewman to arrive at camp after a ten-mile uphill hike and unload from his packsack a dozen railroad spikes, three apples, two neat bundles of dynamite, and a glass bottle of caustic moonshine. These assorted commodities, his personal clothing and gear, and even a few chocolate chip cookies all made the trek in perfect condition, largely because of the strength, roominess and stability of his oversized pack.

In essence, this packsack is a heavy-cotton-canvas box that is designed to fit the Alaskan packboard and carry backpacking gear. Although it is not necessary, you can make the pack larger or smaller or add outside pockets and zipper closures. The accompanying drawings provide instructions for a few simple pockets. Let your imagination and the amount of leftover canvas on hand determine just how elaborate your pack will be.

When carefully constructed, the all-purpose packsack will last for a good many years of hard service. It is probably the most efficient heavy-load pack on earth!

A. The packsack is essentially a canvas box that can be attached to the Alaskan packboard by lacing cord through grommets that match the eye screws on the packboard.

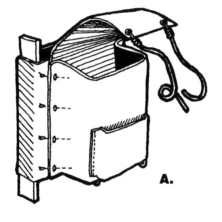

A.

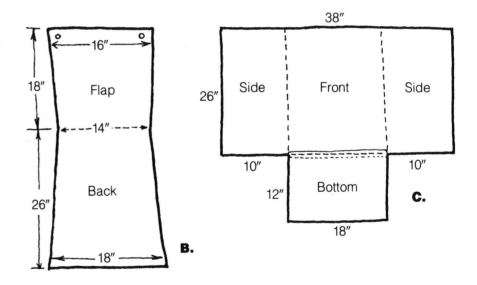

B.

C.

B. First, cut the back and flap of the sack from a single piece of heavy canvas. Double-stitch hem the piece to the dimensions shown. Install 2 grommets at the top of the piece to use for tying the flap down.

C. Cut and double hem the basic body pattern to the shown dimensions. If you cannot find fabric of sufficient size, cut the bottom flap out separately and connect it to the upper piece with a flat-felled seam.

D. Fold the sides into the box shape and double stitch them to the bottom piece. A 2-in. flap remains extended beyond the completed bottom (to help you sew the body to the back).

E. If you add outside pockets, cut them from canvas and sew them to the body piece *before* you connect the body and back pieces of the sack.

F. Join the hemmed body (with 2-in. flaps all around) to the back piece with at least a double seam. The flap extends above, as shown. Install grommets along each margin of the sack to fit the eye screws on the packboard.

G. Make sure the grommets are large enough to accommodate both the eye screws and the wire, which should be at least 26 in. long. The wire runs down each row on the sides of the pack in order to secure the sack to the board.

H. Sew on 2 fabric loops or d rings to the bottom of the completed sack so you can tie the storm flap down. Tie a pair of nylon cords (each at least 18 in. long) through the flap grommets to secure the entire bundle.

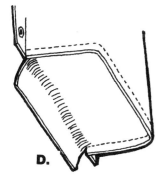

D.

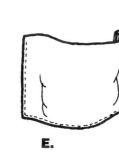

E.

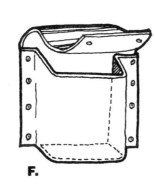

F.

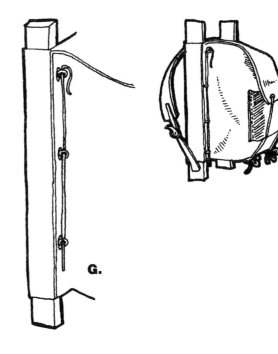

G.

H.

Fanny Pack

The more genteel among us will undoubtedly refer to this simple little day pack as a belt pack, but this is the same gang that refers to underwear as "unmentionables"! As I do not belong to that group, it will be called here, as it ought to be, "the fanny pack."

The design of this particular fanny pack is about as straightforward and logical as it can be. Although there are many exotic designs on the market, a box belt pack is the easiest to make and the most efficient for day hiking. The pack body consists of a nylon box that is large enough to carry a lunch, camera, first-aid kit, or any of the other paraphernalia you ordinarily take on a short hike from a base camp. Because the fanny pack is not expected to carry a particularly heavy load, a light nylon web is strong enough to be used for the belt; an adjustable buckle is attached to it. Just below the top cover, the pack closes with a nylon zipper, which will not corrode.

This pack is my favorite way of carrying gear on the short day hike. It is less tiring than even a small backpack, is easier to get things out of, and is out of the way during a rest stop. Besides, I've got an ample place to carry it!

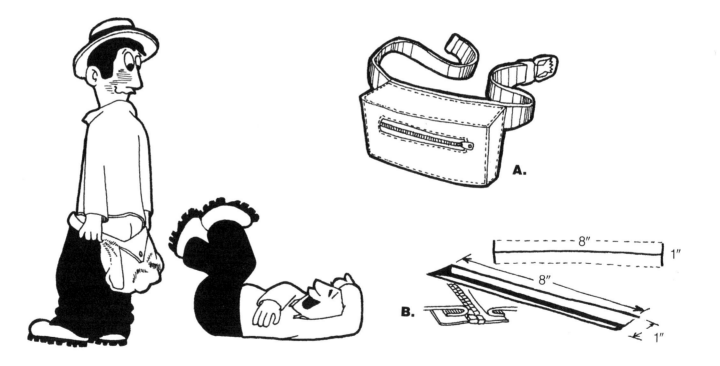

A.

B.

8" 1"

8" 1"

A. Make the entire body of the pack from ½ yd. of coated, waterproof nylon cut to the dimensions shown in fig. D.

B. Before sewing anything, cut the 8-in. zipper hole by merely slitting the material 2 in. below the edge of the top cover and cutting two 1-in. Ts on each end. Fold the flaps under in order to install the zipper, as shown. Make sure the zipper is installed so the seams and edging will end up inside the finished bag.

C. Fold the material to form the box shape. (For simplicity, this illustration shows the box right side out.)

D. Now sew the basic box in the following order. Use plain seams on all edges.

1. Sew the bottom edges to the short side edges (a).
2. Sew the front edges to the long side edges (b).
3. Sew the top edges to the short side edges (c).
4. *Open the zipper.*
5. Sew the top edge to the front edge (d).
6. Push the complete bag through the open zipper. Be persistent until you have the bag right side out and the zipper works.

E. Sew the pack to a lightweight nylon web belt (its length is determined by your circumference) that has an adjustable buckle. Spread the zipper as wide as possible and sew the back of the bag to the belt.

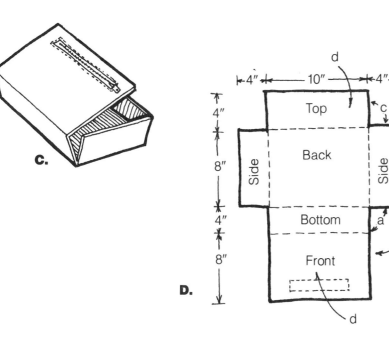

Gaiters

For too long, gaiters have been considered an "elite" piece of equipment. In truth, they are a logical and valuable accessory for hikers of *all* experience levels.

A gaiter is a nylon legging that wraps around a pant leg and provides a water-repellent seal at the boot. The gaiters' primary purpose, of course, is to keep pant legs dry when you are walking through sloppy snow or along a wet, brushy trail. They serve this purpose admirably, yet unobtrusively do a couple of other things as well.

For example, the trend in clothing styles has been flared pant legs, wide cuffs, and bell-bottomed clothing. This is all well and good when we are walking along a concrete sidewalk or a clipped, parklike lawn, but those cuffs and flares too often lead to spills and injuries along the trail. Almost every guide warns against wearing cuffs or bells along the trail, but the fact is, many of us have nothing else in our wardrobe! So, for those of us who wear our stylish duds everywhere, gaiters enclose our ballooning trouser bottoms, thus not only saving us from tripping, but also eliminating the extraordinary amount of water our pant legs absorb along trails.

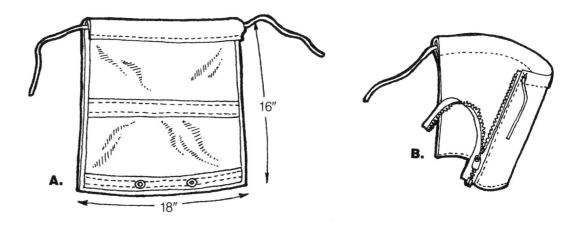

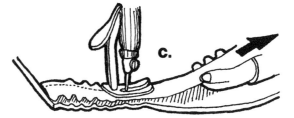

It will probably take you no more than an hour or so to make these gaiters on a sewing machine. For such a meager investment of time and material, you will wonder how you ever got along without them — especially when the rain and the trailside brush combine to make the going difficult.

A. Make each gaiter out of about a 19-in. square of waterproof, rip-stop nylon. Each requires a draw hem top, 2 courses of taut elastic tape, and grommets for a nylon instep cord. Your piece of rip-stop nylon should measure 16 × 18 in. after you have hemmed it and installed the draw hem at the top.

B. Sew the 16-in. heavy-duty nylon zipper in place.
C. Sew 2 pieces of elastic tape to the hemmed gaiter, 1 near the middle and 1 along the bottom margin. As you sew, stretch the elastic tape by hand. The material will pucker behind the needle so that the gaiter will conform to your leg.
D. Install 2 large grommets in the lower elastic course, 3 in. from each side of the garment's center line, and thread the nylon instep cord through them. Place a large lace-hook at the center.
E. Finished gaiter in use. (Note the lace-hook.)

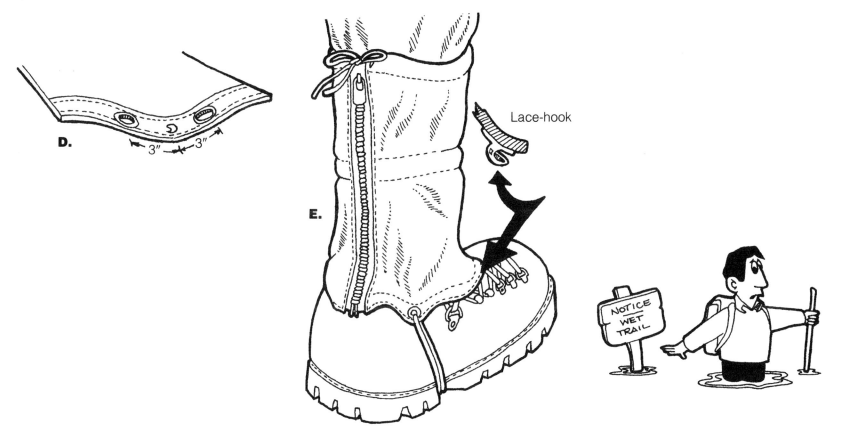

Self-Inflating Air Mattress

The problem of sleeping on the cold, hard ground has apparently been with us ever since our beginning. Wilderness technologists have struggled for years trying to come up with a comfortable solution. After first trying fabric pads, water-filled tubes, ticks of straw, piles of green boughs, air mattresses, and a host of other devices, they devised the foam sleeping pad. It provided limited comfort but did insulate the human body from the cold ground. The air mattress, on the other hand, provided plenty of comfort but almost no insulation from below. Then, somebody decided to combine the best qualities of the two front-runners and thus discovered the solution we had been waiting for — the self-inflating air mattress.

Although the self-inflating mattress is not the easiest project to make, anyone can succeed who will take a little care along the way. The real secret lies in choosing the proper materials and making the critical glue joints *completely* airtight. The latter trick is not so easy as it may sound.

Essentially, the sleeping pad is an open-cell foam pad enclosed in an airtight, waterproof nylon cover. It is made just long enough to support only your head and torso; a larger pad is too cumbersome. The cover is fitted with a small tire valve that allows air to enter or escape. The valve is controlled merely by adding or removing the cap.

The commercially made pads are expensive, but this device can be fashioned at home for substantially less than the cost of the better ones. If you cannot find a good quality coated nylon cloth, look for a used *nylon* air mattress and take it apart. (You will need to separate the inside joints that lie between each mattress tube, but you can manage this without

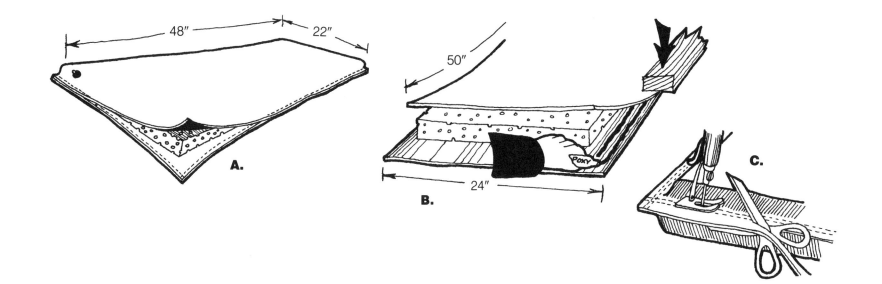

too much difficulty.) In most areas, the proper coated material will be found at yardage or outfitter's stores. Some outdoor catalogs have mail-order material available.

The self-inflating mattress presents some challenge to the home craftsperson, but it is a very comfortable arrangement for trail sleeping. Be sure and carry a spare valve cap so a lost one will not ruin a good night's sleep!

A. Cut a 2-in. thick, open-cell foam pad to 48 × 22 in. *Use only* an open-cell foam pad!

B. Make the cover out of a 50 × 24-in. piece of waterproof, rip-stop nylon. (Buy a coated, pack cloth grade nylon with a chemically bonded agent.) Use epoxy to glue the cover closed; glue as close to the open-cell pad as possible. Spread 2 parallel lines of glue. Place a 2 × 4-in. plank on each seam until it dries.

C. Further strengthen the glued seam by sewing it, using double or triple stitching. *Do not* sew inside the epoxy bond because the seam will allow air to escape. Trim off the excess cover material about 4 in. outside the seams.

D. Purchase a small valve (available at a tire shop) and remove and discard the valve core. Cut a small hole through the mattress cover, place the valve over the hole, and carefully glue it in place. Be sure the joint is airtight. Fit the valve with an airtight cap.

E. When everything is sewn and dry, remove the cap in order to roll the mattress for packing. As you unroll the mattress at camp, it will suck in enough air to fill the open cells and the adjacent airspace in the mattress. Screw the cap back on once it is unrolled.

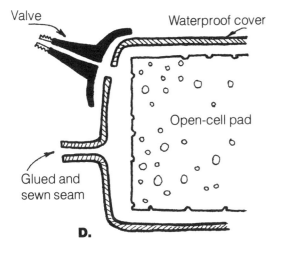

Valve
Waterproof cover
Open-cell pad
Glued and sewn seam
D.

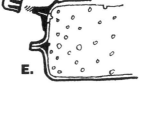

E.

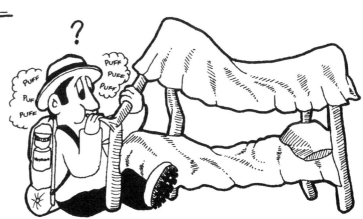

Sleeping Pad

You just cannot overestimate the value of a good night's sleep on any outing, so we have decided to include another sleeping pad. Most of us can manage a two or three day trip with marginal sleeping accommodations, but sleep becomes very important on a longer field excursion. A well-rested hiker can take the tribulations of gnats, crummy cooking, and a summer gully washer in stride, but if a peaceful slumber is impossible because of that familiar rock-under-my-shoulder syndrome, even a broken shoelace is apt to bring tears during the next day's hike.

The secret of undisturbed sleep on the trail is being warm enough (without roasting), being protected from rocks and sticks underneath, and being possessed with a certain prudishness. This sleeping pad will satisfy the first two requirements, but the latter is up to you; that is, if you are serious about undisturbed sleep!

This pad is essentially both a closed-cell and open-cell pad contained within a cover that is waterproof on the bottom but "breatheable" on the top. The two pads are not cemented or otherwise connected, but are kept in place by a fairly tight-fitting cover arrangement. You can also close one end of the cover with a zipper so you can remove the cover for washing.

This double layer pad is not quite so efficient to carry as the

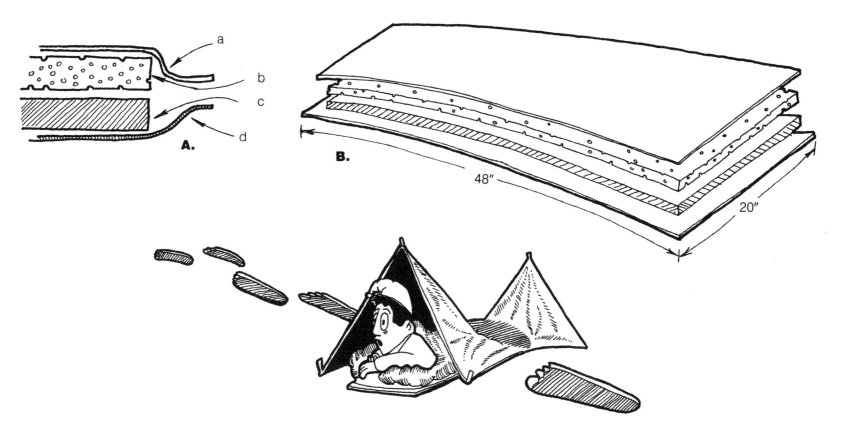

self-inflating air mattress described previously, but it is every bit as comfortable on the trail. With its excellent combination of insulating power and physical support, the sleeping pad makes those trail nights a lot more comfortable.

A. Make the sleeping pad out of 4 basic materials: (a) rip-stop nylon, (b) an open-cell foam pad, (c) a closed-cell foam pad, and (d) coated, waterproof nylon.

B. The pads should be 20 × 48 in. For the lower cover, use a 21 × 49-in. piece of *coated* nylon with the coating placed on the *inside* of the pad. Make the upper cover out of a 49 × 21-in. piece of 1.9-ounce rip-stop nylon.

C. Make 2 roll-up ties out of 2 pieces of 24-in. long nylon tape. Sew the covers up as close as you can get to the pads, adding the ties as you sew the seams. Trim the excess from the edges. If desired, sew a 20-in. zipper at 1 of the narrower ends.

D. Do not roll the pad too tight because the closed-cell foam pad may crack under that kind of pressure.

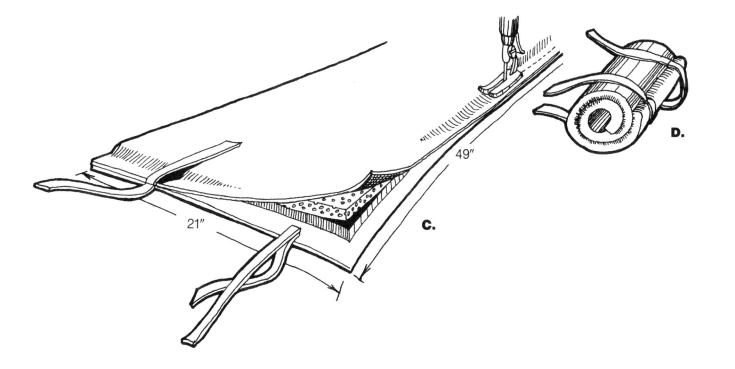

21"

49"

C.

D.

Doggie Pack

There are a lot of pet lovers in this country who shudder at the thought of fixing a special pack for Fido to carry along the trail. Among these are the tenderhearted folk who feel that carrying a pack is cruel and unusual punishment for the dog. Others feel that the cost and labor does not justify the meager load the dog can carry, while others argue that their Fido just is not trained well enough to be trusted with his own pack along the way. Another argument comes from those who contend that dogs should not be on wilderness trails in the first place. This last group may have the ultimate solution.

Certainly a dog can, and usually will, carry his own rations or other items along the trail. A great many breeds were specifically developed as beasts of burden, particularly the husky, malamute, and saint bernard. Many other breeds also respond well to the pack, seemingly happy to add their bit to the family effort. If the dog is too poorly trained to be trusted with a load, he should be kept far from the wilderness trails. Such an animal is a liability to his party and a danger to other hikers who are traveling the same trail.

If your dog is well trained and obedient, and the law allows it, you can include it in your hiking plans by fitting it with a comfortable, custom-fitted pack. The best dog packs are leather or nylon and include padded belly and chest straps. For the dog's comfort, the belly strap should be adjustable. The bellyband we use here is probably the best and most comfortable. The band should fit snugly, but not too tightly — just about the way you would adjust your own belt.

The chest strap is needed to prevent the load from sliding backward off the dog's shoulders. It should never be tightened enough to interfere with the free movement of the forelegs, even if the dog jumps.

The accompanying sketches show an easy-to-make nylon bag that fits most large dogs. This size is ideal for boxers, german shepherds, or collies. Smaller animals, of course, require proportionately smaller

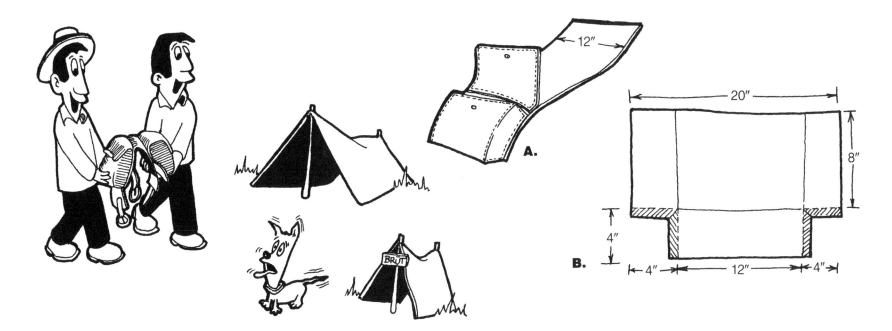

packs. When the bags (made out of nylon pack cloth) are attached, the animal should be able to lie down comfortably with the bags resting on the ground on either side.

Finally, do not overload the dog. A good rule of thumb is to start out with no more than a quarter of his body weight if he is large, less for a smaller breed. The load should consist primarily of the dog's food, so the load is lessened each time he eats. Watch the dog carefully for the first few miles. If the load seems too much (and he is not just balking at carrying *any* load), adjust it as required. With the proper pack and a proper load, Fido can become a valuable and pleasant hiking companion!

A. Make the back support strap out of a heavy nylon strip that is 12 in. wide. (Padded leather can be used.) Measure the distance across the dog's back between his flanks to determine its length. The pack should reach to the flanks on either side.

B. Using the dimensions shown, cut the pack bag front, bottom, and sides out of coated nylon material, pack cloth grade. Note the seam allowance (shaded) at the lower 2 corners.

C. To make the bag's flap, hem a piece of coated waterproof nylon to the shown dimensions. Use double seams to sew the flap to the front, sides, and bottom of the bag. (Follow steps B and C to make the other bag.)

D. Add a few inches to the dog's chest measurement to determine the length of the chest straps. Cut wide heavy nylon or padded leather to this size. Sew a buckle on the end of 1 strap and punch holes in the other strap. Then sew the straps to the back support strap and sew the pack bags on, using double seams.

E. Measure the dog's belly and make the belly strap to fit out of wide padded leather or padded nylon. The smaller buckle straps are sewn outside the big pads as shown.

F. The finished doggie pack

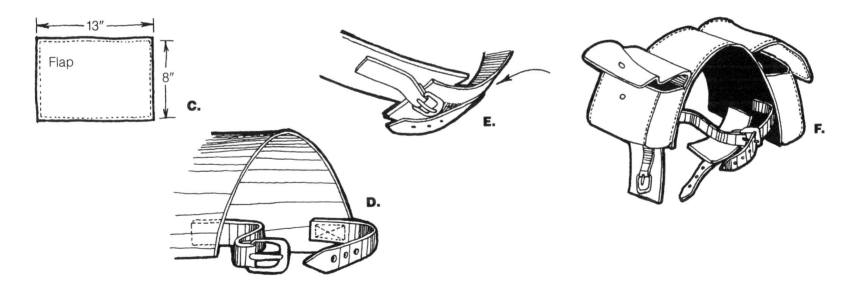

Backpack Tent

By far the most ambitious undertaking in this book, the backpack tent requires considerable sewing dexterity. I have no intention of conducting a mini-course for seamsters or seamstresses here; I just hope to give you adequate directions for putting together a useful, lightweight, and comfortable backpack tent. The two projects following this tent, a rain fly and frost liner, convert this into an excellent four-season shelter that will be useful almost anywhere on the face of the earth. Obviously, you would choose a more substantial dwelling for your final assault of McKinley, and it may be a trifle too warm for a trek across the Sahara, but in most other places it will work just fine.

The reasons for making a lightweight tent at home are many — you save money, you can make it any size your own requirements demand, and you can modify it to fit your own needs. Most important to me, however, is the enormous satisfaction derived from spending a few nights in the wilderness in a tent of my own making. I feel that if I can make everything for myself — and still survive in style — I can handle just about anything this confused society tosses my way.

The tent is a basic wall design with vertical ends and flaps. It is possible to increase the inside space by adding sloping ends and vestibules, but the added labor and difficulty for most of us is not worth the increased space.

The tent is essentially a waterproof box made up of the floor and sidewalls (fashioned out of 2.4-ounce waterproof nylon). To this we add a canopy, a rear wall, and two flaps (all of which are made of 1.9-ounce

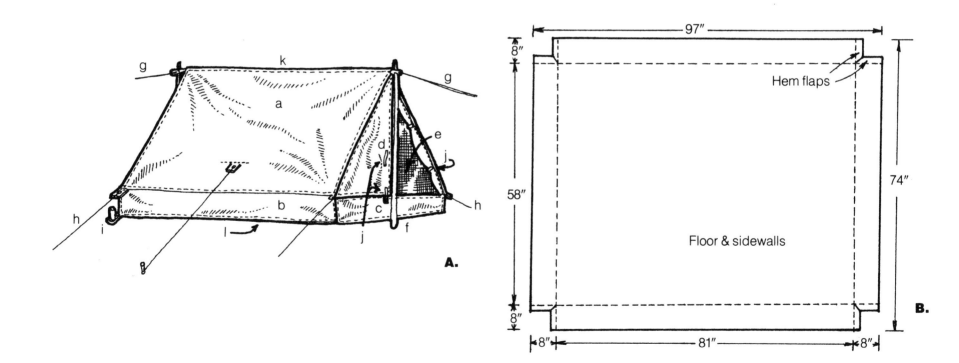

A.

B.

rip-stop nylon). All other aspects of the tent's structure are accessories, such as net lining in certain parts, a window, zippers, and ties.

Once you have completed the construction of the tent, you will need four tent ropes for the sides, four pegs, and two forty-two-inch poles. These can be purchased at an outfitter's shop or fashioned from aluminum or wood. Add two eight-foot lines to each end and attach pegs to each of these.

For handy carrying, roll your newly constructed tent into a neat package and make a nylon utility bag to carry it in. You may also want to make the bag large enough to carry the rain fly, the next component of the tent. Curiously enough, it is also our next project!

A. The backpack tent and its respective parts: (a) canopy, (b) sidewall, (c) sill, (d) storm flap, (e) mosquito net flap, (f) pole, (g) line, (h) rope, (i) peg, (j) tie, (k) ridge, (l) floor.

B. Cut out the 2.4-ounce waterproof nylon floor and sidewalls to the shown dimensions. If you are unable to find a single piece that is 74 in. wide, sew together two 97 × 38-in. pieces with a flat-felled seam (see Chapter 2 for explanations of all seams), and treat the hem with a seam sealer.

C. Fold the sidewalls up and the 1-in. hem flaps (shown in fig. B) in as shown. Before sewing the corners, insert 2 loops of 1 × 6-in. nylon tape for the tent pegs and side lines. Each corner should be triple-stitched as near the outer edge as possible. Be sure to stitch through the hem and loops on each corner.

D. The upper tent is composed of: (a) storm flaps, (b) netting flaps, (c) canopies, (d) end and window. You use 3 zippers and 4 ties to close the front of the tent.

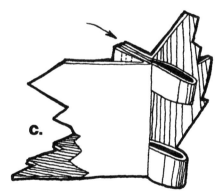

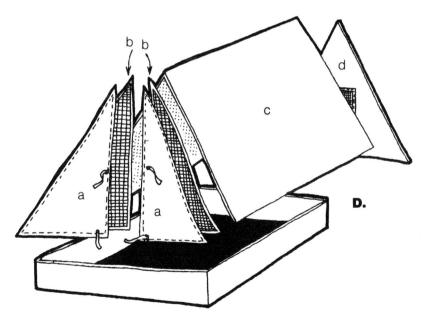

E. Cut out the 1.9-ounce rip-stop nylon upper tent to the shown dimensions. All dimensions are 1 in. larger than finished size to allow for hemming. From the middle of the endwall, cut out a 12-in. square opening for the window.

F. Cut out a 12-in. square piece of netting, sew 1-in. cotton tape around its edges, and sew it over the 12-in. wall opening. Next cut a 13-in. square of 1.9-ounce rip-stop nylon for the storm window flap. Before sewing the upper edge of the storm window flap to the wall

hole, insert two ½ × 12-in. pieces of cotton tape under the upper edge. (You will use these to tie the flap in the rolled, open position.) Sew four ½ × 6-in. ties (2 to the bottom edge of the flap and 2 to the tent) to close the storm window flap. Sew the upper edge of the flap and the 2 ties to the tent.

G. Sew the canopies together at the top with a flat-felled seam that is double to triple stitched for added strength. As you are joining the 2 canopies, sew a 12-in. piece of nylon webbing at each end extending

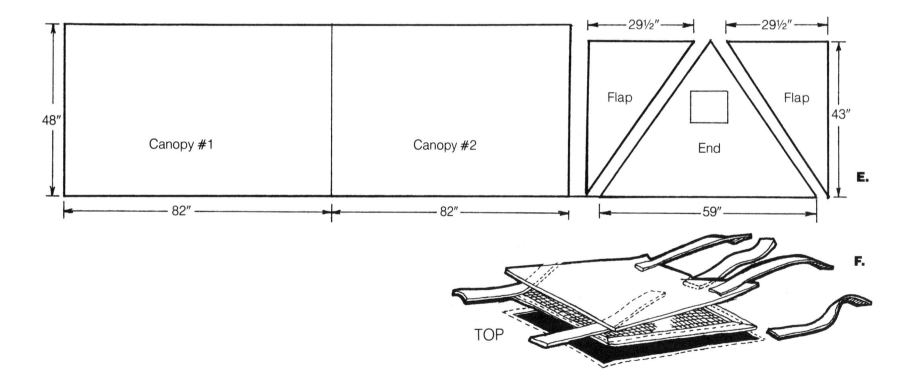

6 in. beyond the canopy. Fit each piece with 2 grommets for the tent poles and support lines.

H. Sew the rear endwall to the canopy sides with a finished hem seam.

I. Flaps — (a) storm flap tied open, (b) netting flap, (c) cotton ties, (d) storm flap. Cut 2 netting flaps (b) to the same size as the nylon storm flaps (see fig. E). Follow these sewing steps:

1. Sew 1-in. cotton tape around each of the netting flaps. Set aside.

2. Hem both storm flaps (d) to 28½ × 42 in.

3. Use a hem seam to sew each storm flap and the corresponding net flap *together* to the inside edge of the canopy. Remember that the storm flap is on the *outside.* As you are making this hem seam, insert three 12-in. pieces of 1-in. cotton tape (c) between the storm flap and the net flap so 6 in. protrude outside the finished tent. You will use these to tie the storm flap open for ventilation(a).

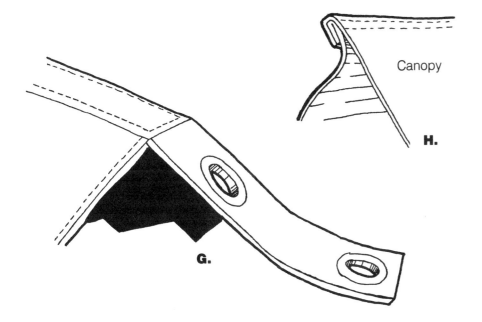

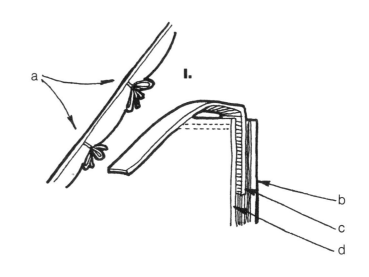

J. Attach the upper tent to the floor/sidewall section. Fold the sidewalls to make a modified insertion seam and sew, using the 2-step sewing process shown. (If you choose to use a hem seam to join the components, make sure the upper tent is sewn to the *outside* of the sidewall material.)

K. Install 3 zippers along the netting flaps. The center zipper attaches the 2 netting flaps together. The bottom 2 attach the netting flaps to the sill (front sidewall). Make sure the zippers close in the direction indicated.

L. Front and rear view of the backpack tent. You can add 2 tape ties to the center of the storm flaps so they can be rolled up. If desired, add a tie at the bottom of each storm flap and corresponding ties to the sill.

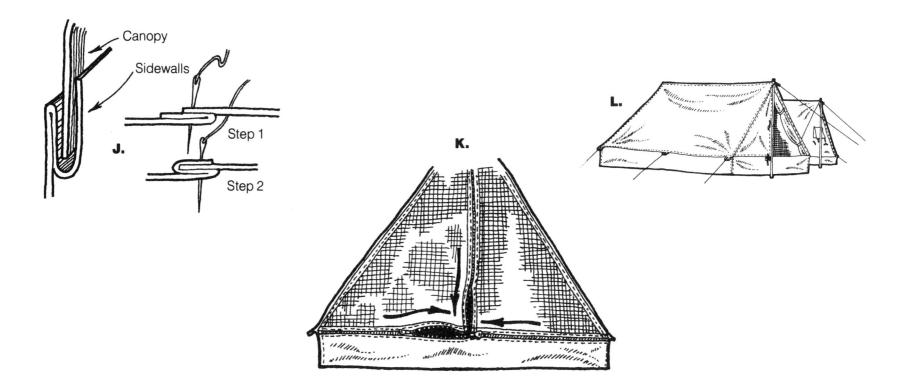

Rain Fly

Without the rain fly, a person would have to be pretty foolish to pitch a tent in any wilderness in North America. Even the desert regions of the country manage to get a little rain when we least expect it.

The fly is a coated, waterproof sheet of nylon that has been custom-fitted to the backpack tent. (You can, of course, alter the dimensions to fit your particular tent.) In practice, the tent is breatheable (that is why we use uncoated, 1.9-ounce rip-stop nylon for that project) and provides protection and comfort inside. If the material were coated, condensation inside the tent would make things pretty clammy, if not unbearable. Unfortunately, the breatheable fabric also lets rain in! The fly, then, allows a layer of air to pass between itself and the tent, providing both rain protection and dry comfort inside.

It is possible to make the tent's fly from a single piece of fabric because material is available in fifty-six-inch widths. It is more economical, however, to buy narrower fabric and sew it together along the ridgeline. Cut the material according to the accompanying pattern. It allows for the sloping overhangs on either end that prevent rain from blowing in through the flaps or window.

It is a good idea to carry eight separate tent pegs, the attached nylon cords, and the proper number of tent rope tighteners for erecting

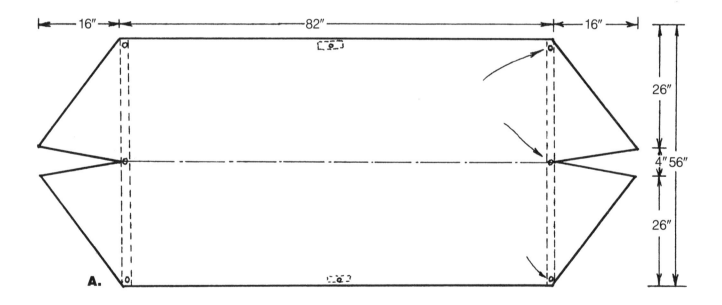

the fly. With the addition of a separate set of poles, you can actually pitch the fly as an open-air shelter when the weather is warm and the mosquitoes are not particularly aggressive!

The fly weighs something like fifteen ounces — scant enough for the enormous degree of protection it gives the camper and his gear. It rolls into a neat little package (or is packed with the tent) and is worth the extra effort to carry it. You should be able to complete this project in a single evening at home, quite a departure from the time it takes to make the tent it will cover!

A. Cut the rain fly, following the dimensions, from a single piece of *coated* 2.4-ounce rip-stop nylon. If you use 2 pieces, connect them at the ridgeline with a flat-felled seam and seal it with seam sealer. Hem the fly all around except *inside* the V-shaped cuts on the ends. Sew the Vs closed, using a plain seam.

B. Sew 1-in.-wide cotton or nylon tape across the fly at each end and along the ridgeline in order to reinforce the areas of stress.

C. Install 10 grommets to help support the fly tent: 2 at the point of each V, 2 at the ends of the ridgeline, and 3 along each side. The end and top grommets go through the fabric tape that has been sewn underneath.

D. Sew a small piece of fabric tape to the undersides of the 3 grommet stress points along each edge.

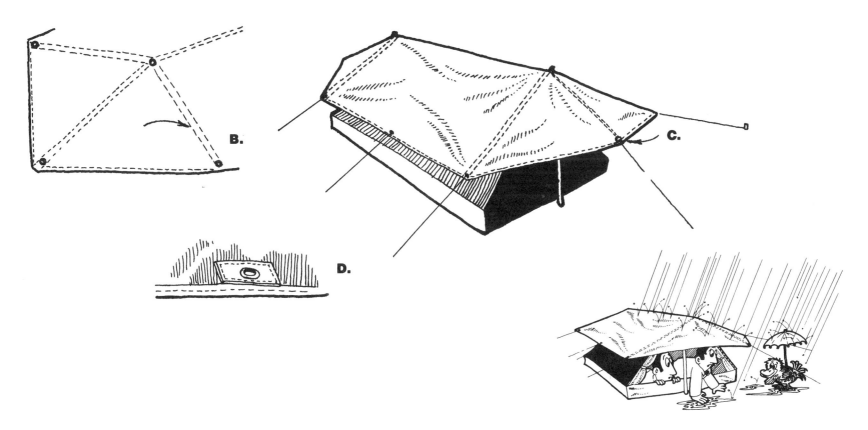

Backpack Frost Liner

The best winter accessories of all, some people say, are a potbellied stove, a roaring fire, and a rocking chair. If one were also to consider a wool afghan, a hot-water bottle, a stiff shot of Ol' Stump Blower, and a romantic companion as *accessories,* the frost liner would surely be way down the list of winter comforts! Actually, most of this list would be thought of as luxuries hardly fitting a stalwart, strong-hearted lover of the wilderness, so the frost liner would probably find itself a trifle higher on the list. Heck, who needs a hot-water bottle?

The liner (generally made of cotton, flannel, muslin, or some other soft, warm, washable fabric) fundamentally acts as a tent within a tent. It is constructed so that it provides a few inches of air space between itself and the outer tent walls and thus serves as insulation to the main tent. The liner is sewn with the seams on the outside (*inside* the tent but *outside* the liner) so the actual construction is simple.

The best way to make an effective liner for a particular tent is to erect the tent as carefully and neatly as possible, get inside with a tape measure and a drawing pad, and try to visualize a two-inch air space all around. Measure the inside dimensions of the tent, subtract two inches, and you have it. (Do not deduct two inches from the floor. There is no way to suspend the liner off the floor!) It is quite possible, of course, to give the proper dimensions for a liner to fit the backpack tent of our previous project, but many readers will be adapting the liner to fit a tent they already have.

The liner is suspended from the inside of the tent by one of several

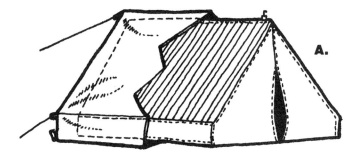

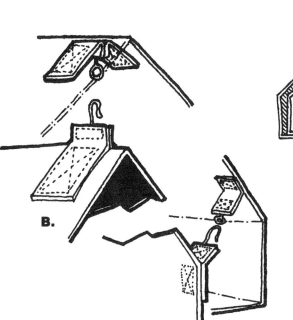

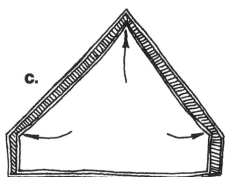

means. You can attach it with a hook and eye arrangement or suspend it with Velcro strips. The second one is a better method because the Velcro holds well during windy periods, and can be reattached during the night without all the fuss and bother of the hook method. Choose the suspension system you think will work best for you and install it. The flaps do not need any attaching devices, and even a sloppy fit will give a high degree of insulation to your present backpack tent.

Remember to allow the liner to have some ventilation. A constant supply of fresh air is necessary, even in the dead of winter. (That is an unfortunate choice of words!) Even the smallest candles generate potentially deadly amounts of carbon monoxide in a tightly enclosed space. If you use a catalytic heater, candle, or lantern inside the liner, leave the flaps *wide open* while it burns. It partially defeats the purpose of the heater, but *cold* is a heckuva lot better than dead!

A. To determine the size of a cotton or flannel liner for your particular tent, measure your tent's inside dimensions (except for the floor) and subtract 2 in. from each measurement. This will give you the appropriate size of each frost liner piece. Cut and sew the liner, using single seams (which will face the roof of the tent), in the same fashion as the pieces for the backpack tent are sewn.

B. Hook and eye sets or Velcro strips are used to suspend the liner from your tent's ceiling and sidewalls (3 sets or strips from the ridgeline and 3 along each sidewall should be enough). The lining floor is in contact with the waterproof tent floor.

C. Suspension points

Field Repair Kit

No single portion of human endeavor is more susceptible to the tenets of Murphy's Law than hiking and backpacking. The portion of the law that states "Anything that can go wrong *will* go wrong — at the most inopportune moment" pretty well sums up the accumulated history of backpacking. Thus, it is essential that anyone who hikes more than sixty yards from the nearest public transportation must outfit himself with an all-purpose field repair kit. By judiciously selecting the tools and materials included in the kit, a clever and resourceful hiker should be able to repair almost anything that breaks down, goes flat, burns through, or otherwise contributes to his misery.

This repair kit is the result of many years of bitter lessons, and it seems to cover most disasters that can occur along the trail. There are bound to be a few that have never been imposed on me, but I am sure time will remedy that. Subsequently, the repair kit is in a state of limbo, waiting for more items to be added.

The carrying case must be replaced every time a major item is added to the kit, so the case is easy to construct and totally expendable. It is made out of light canvas, edged with tape, and sewn into compartments that fit specific items.

Beginning at the right of the illustration, the items in this kit include a plastic vial containing several different needles, which, in conjunction with the spools of thread, can be used for fabric repair. They can patch a torn sleeping bag before the down escapes and mend a small burn hole in the tent.

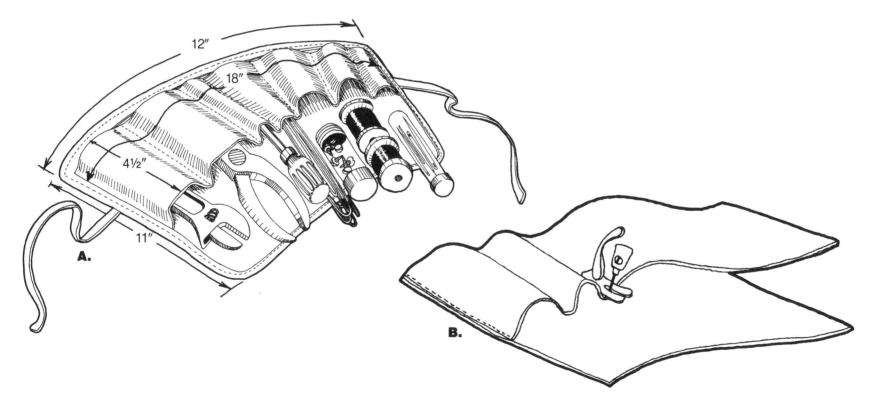

The next vial contains several aluminum washers and an assortment of self-tapping sheet metal screws. These can be used for any number of repairs on gear and cookware. If the cooking pot finally fails under Charlie's instant stew, put a washer on either side of the hole and tighten a large screw through it. The aluminum will bend to fit the inside of the pot, restoring it to at least temporary usefulness.

The small bundle of soft wire can buy a lot of time along the trail — fastening broken frame components, replacing lost pot handles, and a million other things. The screwdriver, wrench, and needlenose pliers are almost indispensable on the average outing, and serve as repair tools, pot lifters, braces, leveling devices, and anything else born out of frustration.

Elsewhere in the pack, I carry a roll of plastic tape, a small tube of cement, and a square of nylon fabric. These items, along with a basic survival kit, should allow you a great sense of freedom and self-reliance on the trail.

A. To make the kit described in this project, use light canvas and cut one 11 × 12-in. back piece and one 5 × 18-in. pocket piece. Hem the pocket piece to make a 4½ × 18-in. rectangle.
B. Sew the pocket piece to the back piece. Stitch down the various compartments to fit the particular tools.
C. Sew 47 in. of wide bias tape around the edges of the kit as shown.
D. Hand sew a 20-in. bias tape tie to 1 end of the kit as shown. Be sure to attach it to only the back piece of fabric.
E. Roll and tie the kit for easy carrying.

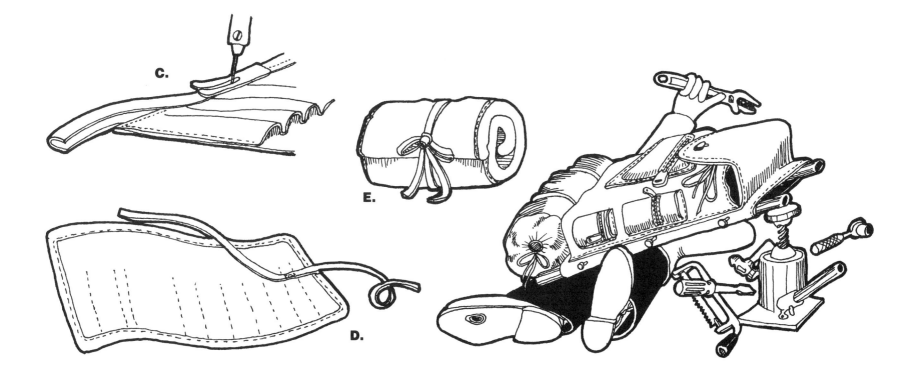

Camera Hitches

This is a valuable gimmick for the camera buff, bird watcher, or binocular-toting hiker. In recent years, several models of the camera hitch have appeared on the market, but judging from the lack of them along the trail, they probably have not been well received. The reason, undoubtedly, is that most of us balk at paying a stinging price for a dollar's worth of elastic and hardware.

The camera hitch is nothing more than an elastic strap that fits around the body, to which is attached a d-ring-and-rubber cradle that holds the camera firmly against your body as you walk. A second strap holds the camera around the neck. (In many cases the original neck strap can be shortened and used in lieu of a specially made support.)

You can purchase d rings and snap-on connectors at most yardage, upholstery, and luggage shops. If surgical rubber is not available locally, it is possible to find rubber strapping or any number of synthetic elastic products to do the job. The surgical tubing, incidentally, is an angling mainstay and should be available in any complete fishing department.

Although the two-strap camera hitch is the traditional model, you can make a more sophisticated device that does not require removing the cradle before using the camera. There is some doubt that the added construction is worth the difference, but the swing-up hitch may suit some people better.

This alternate hitch consists of two elastic arm or shoulder loops that are joined in the back with a suspender tie, as illustrated. The sewing techniques, cradle, and hardware are the same as those used in the simpler model. Make very careful measurements before sewing the

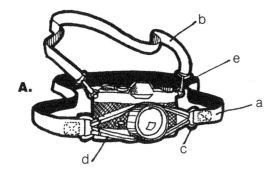

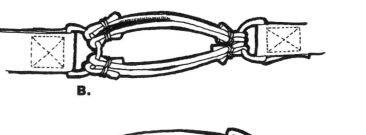

swing-up hitch because the heavier elastic straps do not have the flexibility of the lighter chest strap in the two-piece design. Both are efficient methods for carrying a camera on the trail. Because there is no neck strap, the harness hitch is more comfortable than the other hitch, but the harness may be restrictive when worn over winter clothing or with a backpack.

A. Basic camera hitch: (a) elastic strap, (b) neck strap, (c) d ring, (d) ring-and-rubber cradle, (e) snap-on connectors.

B. Elastic body strap with ring-and-rubber cradle. First measure around the body at the point where the camera will be carried. Subtract 4 in. to determine the length of the elastic body strap. Sew the d ring to the strap as illustrated. Connect 4 strips of ¼-in. surgical tubing to the d rings with twisted wire or tightly tied, woven line.

C. Neck strap. Measure the neck strap after you complete the body strap because it is not made of an elasticized material and must be cut close to the correct length. Then sew 2 snap-on connectors to the ends.

D. To use the basic hitch, remove the cradle from the camera, allowing the cradle and chest strap to remain in place.

E. Front view of variation harness hitch. Use the same sewing techniques, cradle, and hardware as in the first model.

F. Rear view of variation harness hitch. The hitch is composed of 2 carefully measured shoulder straps that are made of elastic material. The 2 are connected in back by a 3- to 4-in. strip of material that is sewn in place.

G. Finished harness hitch

H. To use, swing the camera up to eye level. The harness will slip down in back, allowing the camera to reach the eye position easily.

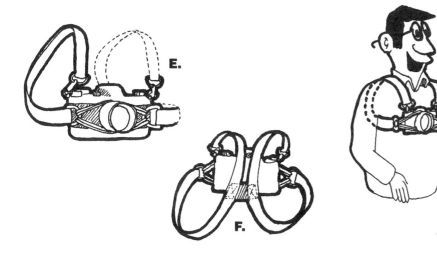

Loss-Proof Sheath

The mystique that surrounds a fine knife is probably another offshoot of the romantic parallels we subconsciously create between ourselves and our pioneering forebears. Yet, aside from this romantic mystique, a good blade happens to be one of the most useful and efficient tools for the day-to-day activities of hiking and camping. It is quite natural that we all eventually quit fooling with those flimsy plastic knives with the beer can blades and break down and buy a truly fine (and costly!) folding knife. Just as naturally, about half of us will lose it!

A clever little sheath for our precious knife can be hand-sewn from the barest scraps of leather. It will keep any kind of knife secure, yet easily at hand for the routine chores of cleaning fish, spreading peanut butter, slicing cheese, paring an apple, and digging the musket ball from the sergeant major's thigh — the usual stuff!

You can purchase the leather expressly for this purpose, or find it in the form of an old purse, jacket trim, or other rummage item. It may be a heavy suede or a finished leather as long as it is sturdy enough to take—

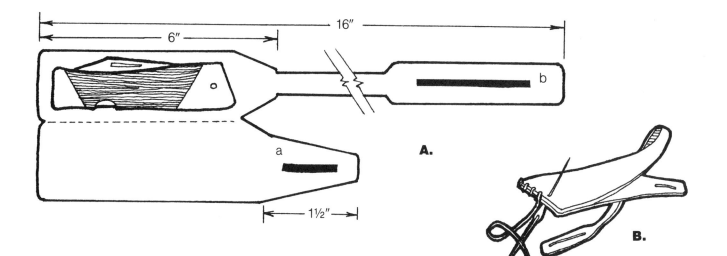

and keep — the stitching.

A hobby-type stitching awl can be used to bind the edge of the sheath, or you can do it with a small punch and a darning needle. Some very thin rawhide makes nice stitching, but a handwoven cotton shoelace will do the job just as efficiently. The resulting pouch receives little stress, so the stitching material is not particularly critical.

As the illustration shows, you loop the sheath around the belt and carry the knife in a hip or front pocket. You can also loop it around a pack frame-member and tuck it into an accessory pocket on the backpack. In either case, it is easy to get at and virtually impossible to lose.

A. To determine the size of the pouch, leave about a ½-in. margin around the knife. Repeat for both sides. Slot "a" is cut about 1 in. long, "b" about 2 in.

B. To form the pouch, fold the sides together and hand-stitch along the bottom and edge. Keep the stitches close together so that the tip of the blade cannot get through.

C. Close by pulling the thong through "a," looping it around the belt, and pulling the pouch through "b."

D. The finished sheath

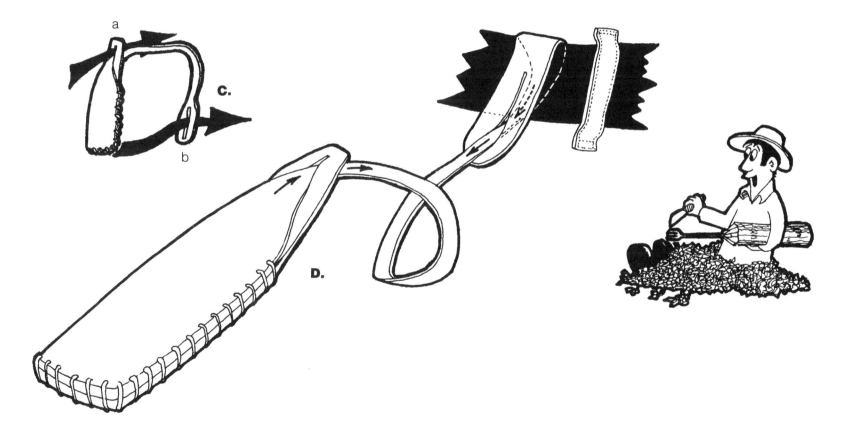

Ax or Hatchet Sheath

Not so many years ago, everybody who ventured into the woods carried either an ax or hatchet. Today the ax probably is not so important as it used to be; the advent of the backpack stove has greatly reduced the need. Still, a lot of people carry and use an ax or hatchet in camp. Despite the growing limitations on campfires, it is likely that the ax will be around for a long time.

Before we get to the nuts and bolts of making a sheath for the ax, let's talk about which instruments to carry in the first place. Ideally, the cutting tool is lightweight, easy to handle, and useful for more than one job. That ideal can be met with either the ax or the hatchet, but when we add safety considerations to our list, the hatchet pales significantly. It is too hard to convert waste wood to usable firewood with a one-handed hatchet. A serious accident can result from too much pressure on a hand that is not accustomed to such work. I prefer, and always recommend, the use of a good camp ax over a hatchet. Whether you choose an ax or a hatchet, be sure to get one with a sturdy sheath. Statistics show us that the list of common wilderness injuries is led by cuts.

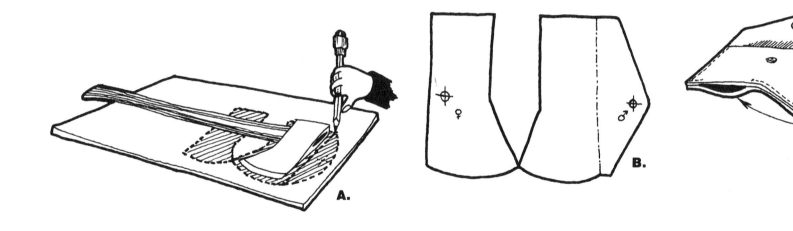

A.

B.

C.

If your ax does not have a sheath — or the one you had mysteriously disappeared — it is not difficult to make a new one. You need a square of heavy leather, access to a strong sewing machine, and a handful of copper rivets. You can find the leather in thrift shops or rummage stores, generally in the form of an old suitcase or valise. If necessary, buy a piece of old belting leather from a machine shop or shoemaker's supply. The sheath need not be fancy, but it must be sturdy. If a person carries an ax in too thin a sheath and then happens to fall, the ax may cut through both the sheath and the victim.

A. Trace an outline of the ax or hatchet on a piece of leather. (You will probably need at least a 12-in. square.) Be sure to double the pattern (to fit both sides of the sheath) and leave a flap to close it.

B. The pattern should look like fig. B when it is cut out, depending on the style of your ax head. Locate the proper spots for the snaps.

C. Sew the edges of the sheath. Be sure to leave a place that is large enough for the handle to pass through easily.

D. Attach soft copper or brass rivets to keep the ax from eventually cutting through the stitching along the front of the sheath. Sew on a snap or buckle so you can close the sheath.

E. The sheath for a double-bit camp ax fits snug in order to provide maximum protection.

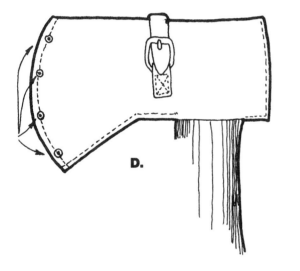

D.

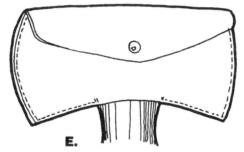

E.

Nylon Utility Bags

An experienced hiker/backpacker is distinguished by the obvious organization he brings into the woods with him. His actions are usually concise and economic; he uses less of his time for chores and more for enjoying the scene he has come to see. In particular, the old hand spends a lot less time rummaging through his pack than does his less experienced counterpart. It seems that he knows where everything in the pack can be found in an instant; he never needs to paw through his clean undies to find the pepper shaker, and can even find a clean handkerchief in the dead of night without using a flashlight — something the novice can't find either!

Not every hiker has a memory that can recall *precisely* where each of the endless gimmicks in the pack can be found, but most of us can greatly narrow the search by providing ourselves with a few custom-fitted utensil bags to tuck into the pack.

In essence, the utility bag is nothing more than an ultralight organizer. It may be a small affair that contains such personal items as a comb, brush, and toothpaste, or it may be a special sack for tucking away cookware and large utensils. In either case, it keeps a particular group of items together so they can be gathered up at a moment's notice.

In addition to having separate bags for each genre of equipment, it is useful to have three provision bags in your pack. The first contains

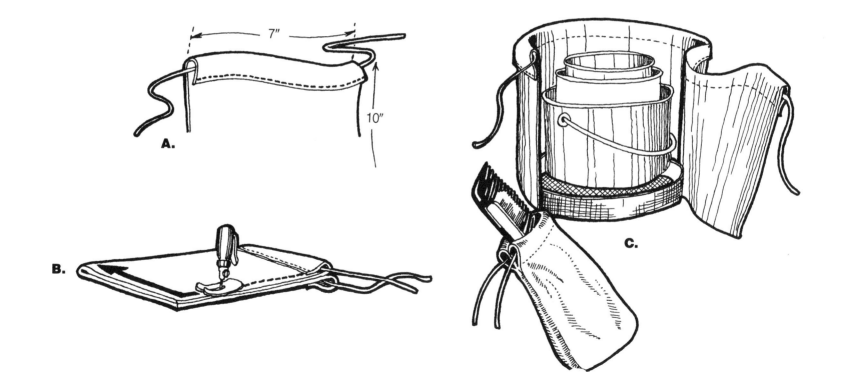

most of the necessary items for either breakfast or dinner (both generally prepared in an established camp), the second for lunches (usually eaten "on the run"), and the third for condiments, cooking aids, drink mixes, and other odds and ends. To avoid confusing a cluttered and limited mind, use different colors for each nylon food bag. Then you need only remember *which* group of foods to put in which color bag, and the rest is relatively easy. The food bags are also easy to suspend from a handy tree during the night — far out of reach of hungry raccoons, curious rodents, and things that go "bump" in the night.

A. To make a toiletry bag, plain hem a drawstring onto a 7 × 10-in. piece of rip-stop nylon.

B. With the draw hem installed, fold the bag, with the inside out, and sew along the open sides as indicated.

C. Turn the sewn bag so the finished side is out and all rough seams are inside, and fill with all kinds of small toilet articles.

D. To make round or oblong-shaped bags, cut and form the bottom with enough fabric turned up to allow for an easy plain hem. Then determine the size of the upper bag by measuring around the bottom piece. As in the simpler bag, plain hem on a drawstring and then sew the bag inside out. Turn the bag right side out when finished.

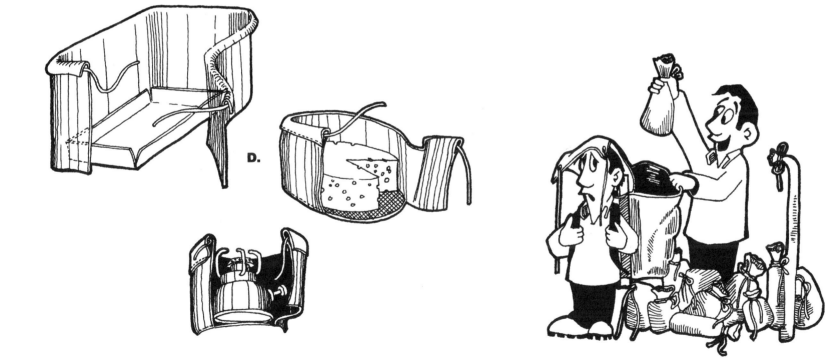

D.

Lantern Caddy

There comes a time in the life of many confirmed backpackers when they forsake the lure of the trail and join the multitudes of recreational vehicles and car campers. This curious, though often temporary, phenomenon generally occurs shortly after the stalwart hiker commits marriage and begins blessing the world with his progeny. While we realize that a few parents are determined enough to go through the ordeal of hauling a tiny human along the trails, we must also understand that they are an overwhelming minority. Most of us take the easier (i.e., vehicular) route. (It is a demonstrated fact that children subjected to the rigors of the trail during their first two years of life will *not* grow into presidents, statesmen, or captains of industry, but they *are* apt to become honest, likable people!) In truth, many great fishing trips or turkey hunts have been conducted solely through this means of transportation, and they have been resoundingly successful.

One of the prime advantages of vehicular camping — children or not — is the ability to take along all the gear necessary for a high level of comfort and activity in camp. Of course, this can also be a disadvantage as the car camper or RV owner must eventually alter his vehicle and his attitude to cope with the problems of stowing and hauling all the junk he has come to consider as indispensable.

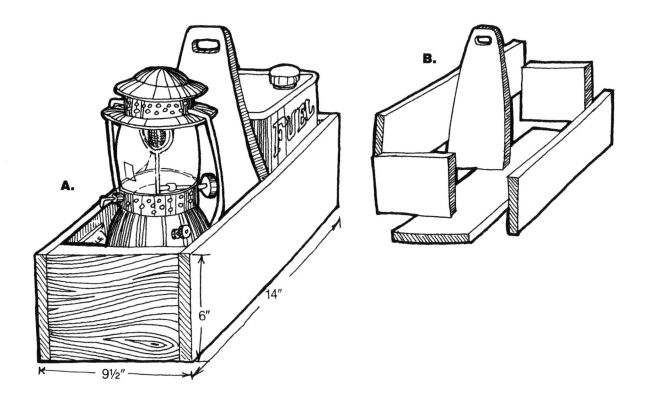

One of the best ways to solve storage dilemmas is to build custom-fitted travel cases for the more fragile equipment. The lantern caddy is such a device, born out of the need to provide the cheery glow of light around the camp, particularly when the kerosene lamp's chimney breaks *again*! This caddy was designed by my father, a man totally familiar with the use and vulnerability of the kerosene lantern!

The carrier is built to the dimensions of the lantern and fuel can you carry. The best bet is to measure the fuel can and build the caddy to fit those dimensions, then pad the other end (with a synthetic foam) for the lamp. In my own device, the lantern end also has enough room to carry a funnel, spare generator, and a couple of packaged mantles. It is easy to pack in the back end of your pickup, keeps the lantern relatively safe from bumps and jars, and is handy when refilling time occurs. The carrier is usually set on end in camp (fuel can down) and acts as a convenient stand for the light.

The lantern companies make some neat shock-proof cases for their products, but they may be costly. This project is low-cost, easy to build, and does the job just fine.

A. The dimensions suggested fit a standard lantern and 1-gallon fuel can. Measure your lantern and fuel can to be sure you have an exact fit.
B. Cut out the carrier's 6 pieces from ½-in. or ¾-in. plywood.
C. Nail the box together. Secure the center handle to the carrier with 1-in. wood screws through both sides and the bottom.

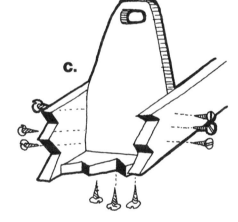

Rock Sample Bag

It seems that the outdoor enthusiast, regardless of his particular persuasion, is an inveterate collector. It is kind of fun to bring home a little memento from a good trip; most of us always find room to tuck away a little piece of volcanic stone, a special chunk of driftwood, or even a few clamshells. You can almost tell the degree of a person's participation in the outdoors by the clutter of knickknacks scattered around the house.

Nobody in the outdoors, however, can match the rock hound when it comes to collecting. Let's face it — seldom is a rock hound content merely to look at a particularly nice rock and then leave it there. If it weighs several tons, he will knock off at least a chip to take back and add to his hoard.

The sample bag here is patterned after an efficient unit I saw up in Alaska a few years back. The prospector (a rock hound who turned pro!) was properly grizzled and salty, and knew his business. He had fashioned his sample bag from a surplus cannon cover (probably the most intelligent use for all cannon covers). The seams were sewn on the outside so little bits and samples would not be lost in the seams. The bottom had a gentle curve, rather than sharp corners, so all the pieces could easily be scooped out at home. Inside the kit were three or four simple little pokes in which he kept small amounts of gold, jade, or other items he wanted to segregate from the chaff.

You make the main portion of this bag from heavy canvas or duck and the shoulder straps out of sturdy nylon web. The straps actually pass under the bag to help support heavy loads. The pokes, which are used for storing collectibles, are made of soft leather — leather that you may be able to cut off an old thrift shop jacket. A short hem on each little

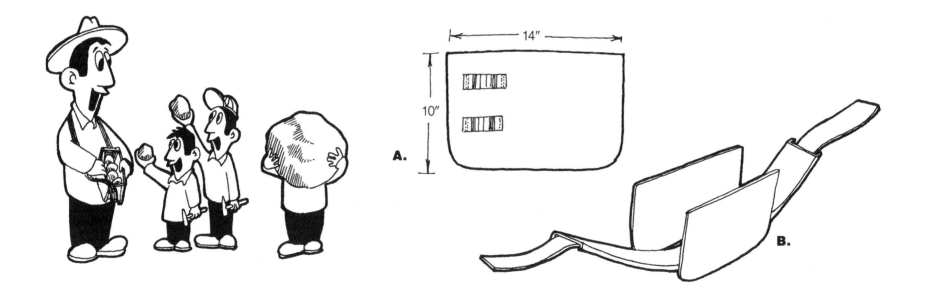

bag provides a handy drawstring closure. It is a fairly simple bag, but about as efficient as you could ask for!

About the closest I ever come to serious rock hounding is fishing with ol' Duane, the granddaddy of all pack rats. We were coming home one time from an evening's rise and I noticed he was limping. I asked him what was wrong.

"Got a rock in my shoe," he answered.

"Why don't you take it out?"

"Can't," he murmured. "It's the best one in my collection!"

A. Cut the 10 × 14-in. front and back panels from canvas duck, as shown, being sure to make a definite rounding of the lower corners. On the front flap, sew on two 1 × 5-in. loops for carrying the rock hammer.

B. Cut the 6 × 34-in. bottom panel out of canvas. Sew the nylon web shoulder strap to the bottom panel so that the strap circles all the way under the bottom and up to form a shoulder strap. (Determine its length by what is comfortable for you.) Attach a buckle within a few inches of the top of the bag after all other sewing is done. Next fold the panel into a U shape as shown and double or triple stitch it to the side pieces. (All seams are on the outside of the bag so they do not obstruct the smooth interior of the bag.)

C. Cut an 8 × 16-in. piece of soft leather for each poke. Sew a 4-in. draw hem on the upper third of the bag, centered on one half as shown.

D. Fold the poke over, stitch the bottom and side openings and turn right side out to use. Number the pokes, which will make recording references easier as you collect.

E. The completed rock sample bag

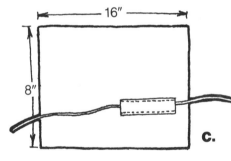

C.

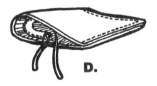

D.

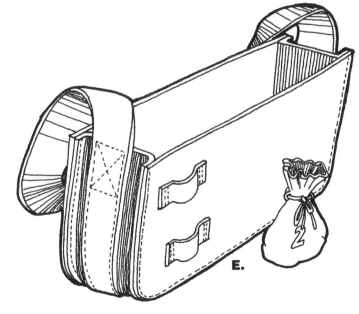

E.

Bootjack and Cleaner

The old-fashioned bootjack, like so many other purely logical gimmicks from another era, has passed from the contemporary scene. For many of these formerly familiar items, the reason for their passing is simple: The primary equipment on which they were used is no longer around. Collar buttons and button hooks, for example, disappeared when society quit using celluloid collars and high button shoes.

The bootjack, however, did not have such a rational reason for dwindling away into memory. If anything, there are more boots around now than there were a half-century ago. It is quite true that many of us do not use our boots on an everyday basis any longer, but they are just as hard to remove now as they were then. The simple little bootjack deserves at least a shadow of its former significance on the back porches of America!

The jack is constructed of almost any old scrap of wood that is strong enough to stand on. The wood is sawed into a V at one end so that it is narrow enough to catch the heel of the boot. To operate it you merely stand on the jack with one foot, engage the heel of the boot on the other foot, and pull up your leg. The boot slides off with remarkable ease!

Of perhaps greater import — especially to a family with kids and a nearby source of dirt — is the almost-automatic shoe and boot cleaner. This miraculous device consists of three stiff-bristled scrub brushes (what do you mean, you don't remember what those are?) affixed to uprights on a platform of lumber. The person using the cleaner can stand on the end portion of the board while cleaning his boots without the darn

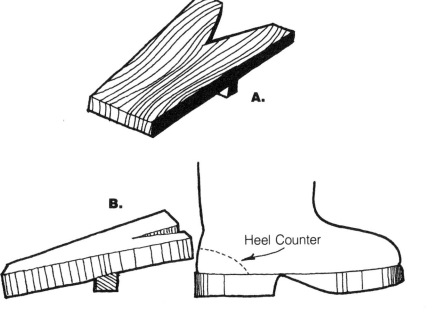

A.

B.

Heel Counter

thing skittering all over the floor. (This is obviously important, especially if you are acquainted with what havoc childlike exuberance can cause.) Kicking a foot through the bristle "channel" formed by the brushes on the board removes all the dirt from the shoe or boot, even that along the welt and edges.

The jack and bristle cleaner are both relics of an earlier age, but they should not be considered old-fashioned. They are both perfect for the lakefront vacation cottage, but do not overlook them for full-time use at the family homestead. They are a darn sight better than the best welcome mats — especially around a dairy farm!

BOOTJACK

A. The best size wood for constructing the bootjack is a 6 × 12-in. piece of ¾-in. plywood. In 1 end, saw a V that is narrow enough to catch the heel of your boot. Nail a small piece of wood onto the jack's underside to elevate it slightly.

B. To operate, stand on the jack with 1 boot, insert the heel of the other boot in the V, and pull up.

BOOT CLEANER

C. Screw two 2 × 6 × 4-in. pieces of board (size can vary depending on the size of the brushes you use) near the center of a 2 × 6 × 24-in. board. Gauge the distance between the 2 upright boards such that the 2 side brushes will touch the middle brush once they are installed.

D. Using long wood screws and starting from the bristle side, secure the 2 stiff scrub brushes to the uprights and a third scrub brush to the baseboard. You may have to drill holes in the brush handles before screwing them.

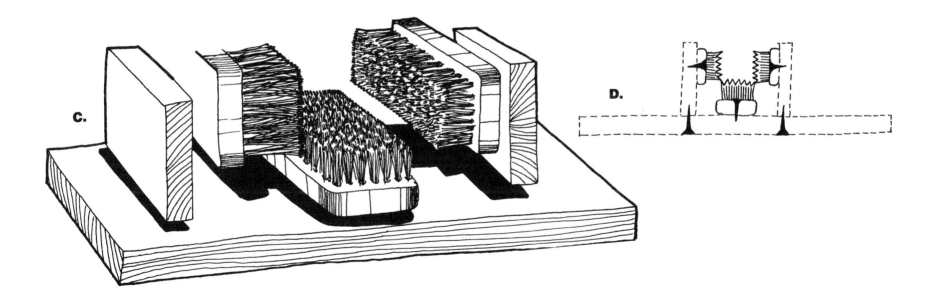

Boot Hanger

This is one of those simple little devices that really does a good job, takes only a dime's worth of wire, and can be made in a matter of minutes. We each could probably go out and buy one for half a buck, but (unless we already have one) the lack of cost or the little effort required obviously has not made any difference to us. Our hip boots are stuffed in the bottom of the closet, our hiking boots were probably put away damp, or we are now facing the prospect of replacing a pair of boots that wore out too soon (as will those hip boots and hiking boots we put away improperly). If this little project can persuade any of us even to *buy* a simple hanger for our boots, it will have done us a great service!

In the case of hiking boots, of course, a season's wear and tear can be pretty tough. Periodic replacement of these is inevitable, but good care still helps. A good pair of hip boots or waders, on the other hand, probably should *never* wear out. It is abuse, rather than wear, that relegates most rubber hip boots to the junk pile.

By way of illustration, I can cite my father's favorite steelheading boots. They are an old pair of rubber-over-fabric boots that have not been made for at least forty years. Still, whenever we go fishing I notice that I am sporting another new pair of boots while he is slogging along in a pair that is nearly as old as I am. It is not that he is any easier on his boots than anyone else. He wades the toughest rivers, digs his share of clams, and has hunted ducks, trimmed ditches, and dug septic tanks —

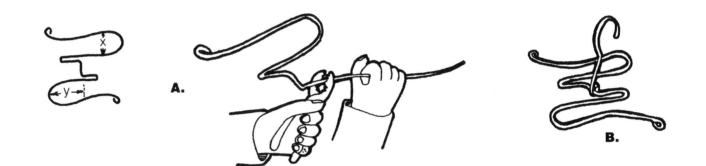

all in that same pair of boots.

The answer, of course, is that he takes good care of them *after* he uses them. He thoroughly washes his boots after every heavy outing, never puts them away wet, and hangs them under the stairway where they belong. The point in all this is simple: If we had adopted the proper attitude toward our gear (and the money it costs!), we already would have had a hanger to keep those boots in top shape.

The hanger is bent from wire in such a manner that it adapts to almost any boot and also folds flat for carrying. The boots hang sole upward, allowing the moisture inside to evaporate quickly and naturally. When drying hiking boots this way, be sure to keep them away from direct heat, even that of the campfire. Nothing will age or damage the material faster than overdrying after a thorough soaking, so use a little patience when drying your shoes and boots. They will last a lot longer and serve you better while they are around.

A. Make the hanger by bending 3 ft. of wire. Be sure that dimension x on each side is narrow enough to grip each boot firmly, and that dimension y is equal on each side for proper balance.

B. For a hanger, fashion a wire hook out of a short piece of wire.

C. Make the clamping loops of the hanger narrow enough to fit below the heel reinforcements of your boots; the soles are held upright. Remember never to dry boots by direct heat.

Canoe Paddle

There are few wilderness activities that can match canoeing as a purely individualistic endeavor. Certainly, many waterborne travelers choose a companion on their journey, but at least a few paddlers enjoy traveling solo on the long canoe trails of this country. Even more than the long-distance hikers or backcountry fishermen, these singular souls and their frail crafts epitomize absolute freedom. Even if your canoe activity is of a more gregarious nature, you can feel accomplished and have fun by making some of the gear at home. Except for the canoe itself, what major piece of gear could be more practical and mean so much to the user as a custom-made and personally fitted paddle?

Before starting this project, it is important to decide what size and shape your personal paddle should be. The rule of thumb for length, of course, is that the paddle should reach from the ground to a point halfway between your chin and eye. In practice, you may find a slightly longer or shorter one suits you better.

The blade shape and size are determined in large part by how strong you are and how frequently you will be paddling. Generally, a wider blade takes a great deal more strength to use because it moves proportionately more water than a narrow blade; yet the wider blade has the advantage of being more maneuverable than a narrow one. Most people eventually settle on a compromise — a paddle from five to eight inches broad. I prefer an eight-inch blade for most purposes, but use a wider paddle on "soft" lake water.

Once the size has been determined, you can design your paddle. The accompanying sketches are for a laminated paddle, which gives you a strong shaft and a light blade. A paddle cut from a single board of hickory or ash, of course, is tough but it is also heavy. Using softer woods in the laminations reduces the blade weight considerably.

The center shaft or handle should be seasoned, straight-grained hardwood. The inner blade laminations should be seasoned fir, hemlock, or other medium density wood. The outer laminations, which will become the blade edges, should also be hardwood. They will eventually take a beating from rocks, landing docks, and other hazards.

The paddle should not be varnished or painted, although a majority of the commercial models are. Instead, rub boiled linseed oil into the wood with your bare hands. The oil is available at any paint store and will

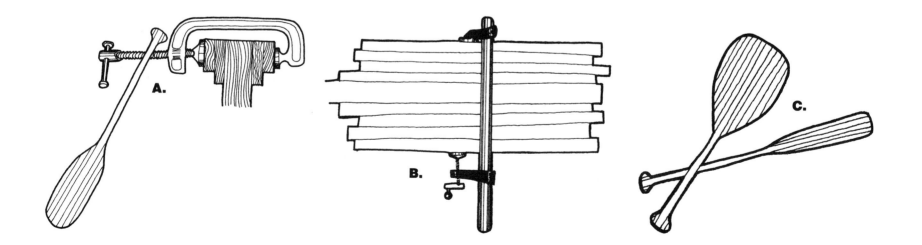

A.

B.

C.

properly season the wood without the hard finish associated with varnish and polyurethane. The varnished paddle becomes heated and blisters a lot more quickly than an oiled one.

This woodworking project will produce an outstanding paddle, one that you will be happy with for years to come. Who knows? If you do a good enough job on the paddle, maybe you will be tempted to tackle something really big. A few weeks in the garage, a little guidance from books and other canoeists, and perhaps next season you will be (pardon me, I can't help it) *paddling your own canoe!*

A. After sizing your paddle according to the text suggestions, select a 1¾-in. block of seasoned, straight-grained hardwood for the center shaft (handle).

B. Cut several pieces of 1 × 2-in. wood (use medium-density wood for the inside and hardwood for the outside laminations) for the blade laminations. Make sure they are long enough to form the completed blade. The number of laminations depends on the desired width of the final blade. Glue the laminations in their proper position (the 2-in. sides of the boards are glued together) with a good grade cabinet glue. Clamp them firmly in place for at least 48 hours before releasing.

C. You can design anything from a fan to a long white-water blade with this lamination process.

D. Roughly shape the laminated block with a jig or band saw. You must rough out the blade for thickness and cross-section shape before you do the final sanding and shaping. Then use a good belt sander to speed up the shaping process.

E. Make the handle knurl by laminating two 1-in. pieces of soft wood to both sides of the handle blank. After drying, shape and sand the glued block as a single piece. (Follow laminating and shaping instructions in steps B and D.)

F. Bring the handle blank (1¾-in. square) to a comfortable size after you have roughed in the blade and handle knurl. A comfortable size is usually around 1⅜ to 1⅝ in. Start the blade taper 6 in. above the shoulders of the blade (see fig. D).

G. Taper the finished blade from shaft to tip and from side to side. Too blunt a blade causes excessive drag. Do any finishing sanding that needs to be done.

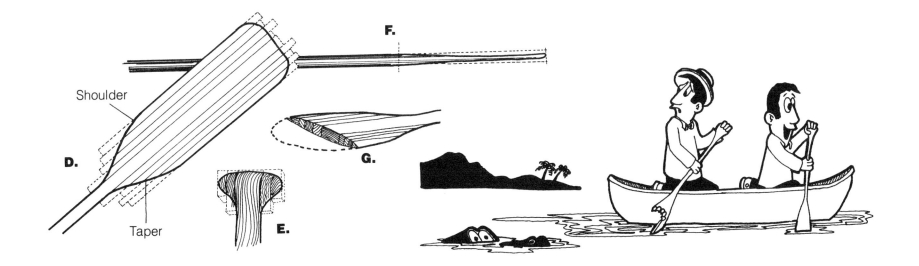

Shoulder

F.

D.

Taper

E.

G.

Turkey Call

Of all the confusing, mysterious, and downright frustrating pursuits that the outdoors has to offer, none can quite match the ancient and honorable sport of hunting turkeys. Now, hunting turkeys is not the same as hunting deer, caribou, or gazelle because, you see, *hunting* turkeys does not necessarily mean *shooting* turkeys. In fact, the vast majority of turkey hunters never even take a shot at one.

By way of explanation, let me relate my own experience as a hunter of the turkey, one of the wiliest of all wild animals. Every year, I take a pilgrimage to the turkey country of the Pacific Northwest, usually accompanied by ol' Duane and his brother Zeke. On a typical hunt, we spend three or four days in one of the most beautiful oak rangelands in the country, eat the finest of trail fare, wash it down with branch water and the world's worst coffee — and thoroughly enjoy the whole affair. We make heroic attempts to lure the turkey within sight, but the simple fact is — none of us has the slightest intention of shooting one of the most beautiful and majestic of game birds. You see, the fun is in the *hunt,* not the *harvest!*

Calling a turkey takes a great deal of practice, patience, dedication, and one of the silliest contraptions you will ever consider building. Yet the thrill of actually coaxing a strutting tom within camera range is an experience that no outdoorsman should voluntarily deny himself. It is fun!

As can be seen from the accompanying sketches, the turkey call is a model of simplicity. It consists of a hollow cedar box (whittled to a fairly close tolerance), a movable (preferably mahogany) hardwood paddle, and a bit of chalk to make it squeak. Once it is put together, its effec-

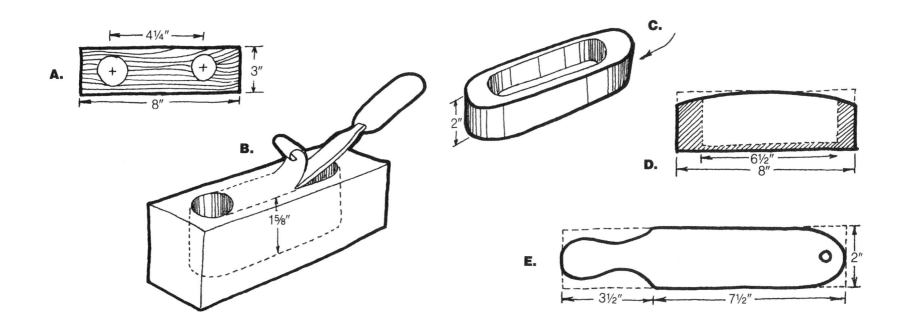

tiveness is simply a matter of technique.

To operate the call, liberally chalk the upper sidewalls and the part of the paddle that touches them. Draw the paddle gently sideways across the sidewall and the resulting sound will be akin to drawing your fingernails across a blackboard. It may make your teeth hurt, but to a lovesick tom turkey it is pure ecstacy! To polish up your technique, it may help to visit a turkey farm. Then, with a little practice, you will be able to duplicate the yelp, cluck, and feeding chatter of a wild turkey. Once this is mastered, you will be able to call in one of the most splendid sights in all the wild — the strutting, mating-minded tom turkey. Maybe!

A. Drill two 1¼-in. holes (at the points shown) in a 2 × 8 × 3-in. piece of cedar. Drill 1⅝ in. deep.

B. Using a small wood chisel, remove the wood between the holes to a depth of 1⅝ in. Smooth and sand the resulting cavity until it is straight and smooth.

C. Now carve and sand the bottom and sidewalls to precisely ⅛-in. thicknesses. The thicker ends of the box should be about ¾ in.

D. Again using sandpaper, taper each top end of the wooden "bathtub" about ½ in. below the original dimension. When all is smooth, the body is done.

E. Make the paddle out of an 11 × 2 × ½-in. piece of mahogany that is sanded to the dimensions shown. Drill a ³/₁₆-in. hole near the end.

F. Shape the paddle with sandpaper to slightly round the bottom. The cross section should be a flat "boat" shape, about ⅛ in. thick at the outside.

G. Attach the paddle to the body with a ⅛ × 1½-in. flathead wood screw.

H. Turkey call in use

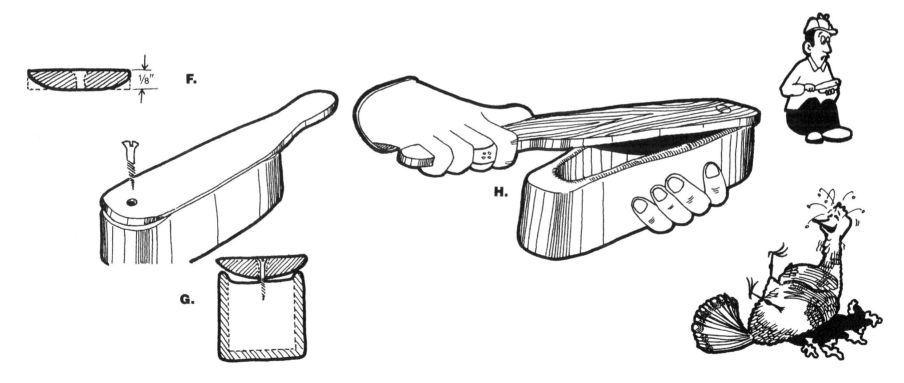

F. 1/8"

G.

H.

Alpenstock

In the Glory Days of Hiking (i.e., prior to the invention of the confounded trail bike!), there was hardly a soul that would venture along even the nearest of trails without a sturdy alpenstock in hand. Ranging from a primitive stick to an inlaid staff of ironwood and teak, the alpenstock was the outward sign, the very symbol, of the recreational walker. It quietly signified that here was a person of leisure, a stroller along nature's pathway. It meant that the bearer was on the trail by choice, and was not a woodsman, a rough logger, or a hobo seeking the nearest railhead. In short, the alpenstock was a badge of status to be enjoyed by those who could afford the time away from the serious business of existing in a cruel world. But somewhere along the line, the alpenstock fell by the wayside and then was carried by only old fuddy-duddies, who occasionally blocked the way of the young, fashionable, ice-ax toting newcomers to the trail.

It is not really the passing of the alpenstock that is mourned so much as the dawning of a new era in hiking, an era marked by the ever-increasing desire for longer trails, faster times in crossing them, and better and sometimes finer equipment (with the labels on the outside, naturally). I suppose it is just a case of whistling up the wind to wish that a calmer, quieter mood could again prevail along the trails.

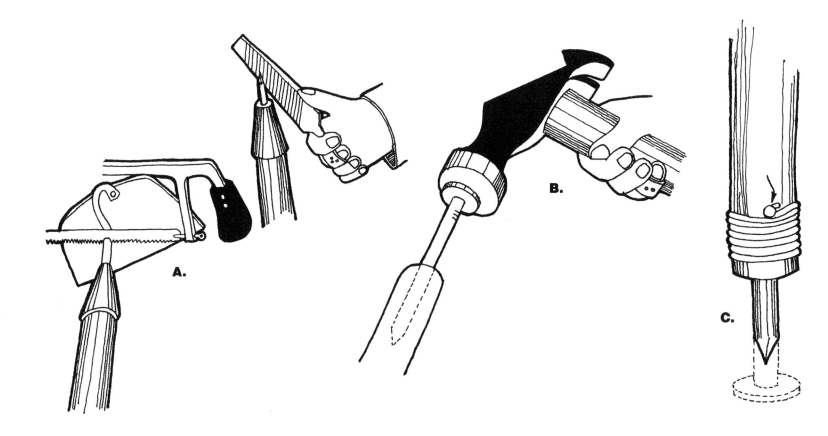

A.

B.

C.

The inclusion of the alpenstock in this book is maybe just my way of urging you to rediscover — with this strange old symbol — the greatness of the wilderness that my father knew. Maybe you did not have a friend like my father who could bring the forest alive for you and teach you the wonder and respect it inspires. Perhaps the alpenstock is my way of passing his message along to you.

How do you make one? Just look at the drawings; it's a cinch. *Why* would you make one? Ah, there's the question!

A. You can make a good alpenstock from an old hoe. Cut the head off and file the remaining shaft into a short, sharp point.

B. You can make another walking staff by driving a twelvepenny spike into a hardwood shaft.

C. Cut off the nail's head and sharpen the remaining end. Wrap the end of the staff with soft wire to prevent it from splitting. Wind the wire's end around a small nail. Pound the nail into the shaft.

D. A traditional staff can be made from a sturdy vine maple, ash, hickory, or other hardwood limb. Whittle the end to a sharp point.

E. To harden the whittled end, put it over the fire just until the wood chars. Remove it, scrape off the charred material, and then repeat the process 2 or 3 more times.

Other Books from Pacific Search Press

COOKING

Asparagus: The Sparrowgrass Cookbook by Autumn Stanley. Over 100 ways to serve the low-calorie, nutritious vegetable of kings. Includes helpful tips on cultivation. Drawings. 160 pp. $3.95.

Bone Appétit! Natural Foods for Pets by Frances Sheridan Goulart. Treat your pet to some home-cooked meals made only with pure, natural ingredients. Recipes fit for both man and beast! Drawings. 96 pp. $2.95.

The Carrot Cookbook by Ann Saling. Over 200 mouth-watering recipes. Drawings. 160 pp. $3.50.

The Crawfish Cookbook by Norma S. Upson. Try the lobster's freshwater cousin, the crayfish, for inexpensive gourmet dining. Over 100 recipes for every time of day. Drawings. 160 pp. $3.95.

The Dogfish Cookbook by Russ Mohney. Over 65 piscine delights. Cartoons and drawings. 108 pp. $1.95.

The Green Tomato Cookbook by Paula Simmons. More than 80 solutions to the bumper crop. 96 pp. $2.95.

Wild Mushroom Recipes by the Puget Sound Mycological Society. 2d edition. Over 200 recipes. 176 pp. $6.95.

The Zucchini Cookbook by Paula Simmons. Revised and enlarged 2d edition. Over 150 tasty creations. 160 pp. $3.50.

CRAFT

Spinning and Weaving with Wool by Paula Simmons. Over 20 years of experience enables the author to help you become a successful spinner and weaver of wool. 162 black-and-white photographs, 76 technical drawings, 33 line drawings. 224 pp. $9.95; $17.95 (cloth).

NATURE

Butterflies Afield in the Pacific Northwest by William Neill/Douglas Hepburn, photography. Lovely guide with 74 unusual color photos of living butterflies. 96 pp. $5.95.

Cascade Companion by Susan Schwartz/Bob and Ira Spring, photography. Nature and history of the Washington Cascades. Black-and-white photos, maps. 160 pp. $5.95.

Common Seaweeds of the Pacific Coast by J. Robert Waaland. Introduction to the seaweed world — its biology, conservation, and many uses for both industry and seafood lovers. 42 color photos; diagrams, illustrations. 136 pp. $5.95.

Fire and Ice: The Cascade Volcanoes by Stephen L. Harris. Copublished with the Mountaineers. Black-and-white photos, drawings, maps. 320 pp. $7.95.

Little Mammals of the Pacific Northwest by Ellen Kritzman. The only book devoted solely to the Northwest's little mammals. 48 color and black-and-white photos; distribution maps, index. 128 pp. $5.95.

Living Shores of the Pacific Northwest by Lynwood Smith/Bernard Nist, photography. Fascinating guide to seashore life. Over 140 photos, 110 in color. 160 pp. $9.95.

Messages from the Shore by Victor B. Scheffer. Noted naturalist and author gives his testimonial to the beauty and meaning of the saltwater beaches. 51 color photos. 80 pp. $8.95.

Minnie Rose Lovgreen's Recipe for Raising Chickens by Minnie Rose Lovgreen. 2d edition. 32 pp. $2.00.

Sleek & Savage: North America's Weasel Family by Delphine Haley. Extraordinary color and black-and-white photos; bibliography. 128 pp. $5.50.

Why Wild Edibles? The Joys of Finding, Fixing, and Tasting – West of the Rockies by Russ Mohney. Color and black-and-white photos, illustrations. 320 pp. $6.95.